PEKINGESE

A Practical Guide for the Pekingese Lover

Jenny Drastura

Pekingese

Project Team
Editors: Heather Russell-Revesz,
Stephanie Fornino
Indexer: Joann Woy
Design: Jenn Martino

TFH Publications®
President/CEO: Glen S. Axelrod
Executive Vice President: Mark E. Johnson
Editor-in-Chief: Albert Connelly, Jr.
Production Manager: Kathy Bontz

TFH Publications, Inc.®
One TFH Plaza
Third and Union Avenues
Neptune City, NJ 07753

Printed and bound in China
14 15 16 17 18 19   1 3 5 7 9 8 6 4 2

Library of Congress Cataloging-in-Publication Data
Drastura, Jenny.
  Pekingese / Jenny Drastura.
      p. cm.
  Includes index.
  ISBN 978-0-7938-4186-8 (alk. paper)
  1. Pekingese dog. I. Title.
SF429.P3D73 2012
636.76--dc23
                              2012002862

The Leader In Responsible Animal Care For Over 50 Years!®
www.tfh.com

Table of Contents

Chapter 1

History of the Pekingese

There are many accounts of "small," "short," and "square" dogs in Chinese history and art as early as 1760 BCE. A small statuette of a snub-nosed mastiff, its tail curved over its back, was unearthed from a Han tomb (25–220 CE). This dog is believed to be a descendant of the Tibetan wolf, which led to many breeds, including the miniature breeds of China so popular in Tang (618–970 CE) times, and on to the toys of the modern era.

Throughout history the little dogs have had varied roles, some magnificent, some tragic. According to surviving records from the Chou Dynasty (about 1027 BCE–221 BCE), stout little canines with compressed noses were coveted by the Chinese Imperial court, which demanded them as part of the yearly tribute from the southern provinces, along with amber, pearls, ivory, rhinoceros horns, and kingfisher feathers. For many centuries the surest way to an emperor's heart was to present him with a dog.

Around 500 BCE, an eyewitness describes small pampered canines with distinctive short mouths who were carried in the chariots by their aristocratic masters while larger, longer-mouthed hounds followed alongside. Sadly, dogs were also used as protein for the Chinese diet, and for sacrifice. Dogs were often killed and buried under the main gates of the temples to ward off evil. Whether these small, short-mouthed dogs were even close to the modern Pekingese is anyone's guess, but it is clear that dogs were a major part of Chinese culture.

Chinese dogs as we know them probably began to take shape during the early Han Dynasty (206 BCE–220 CE), when two major trade routes carried silk from China to Rome and Greece in exchange for toy dogs, fighting dogs, and hunting dogs, as well as other animals and treasures. These toy dogs included the long-haired Melitaei, or Roman Maltese, and were probably part of larger cargos of fine textiles and perfumed oils. It is known that two

The Pekingese originated in China, where the breed was raised in the lap of luxury.

THE FABLE OF THE PEKINGESE

"The Story of the Lion and the Monkey and how the Pekingese came to be Legend" has it that a lion once met a marmoset, a small monkey, and desperately fell in love with the little creature. The lion prayed to the Lord Buddha to make him small enough to court his true love, at the same time begging that he might retain his great heart to love her with. The Lord Buddha granted his prayer and turned him into a Pekingese, changing his stature alone, leaving him his lion form, his intrepid courage, and above all, his mighty heart. The Lion Dog also inherited the impudent face, the intellect, and the sense of the monkey!

dogs, a male and a female matching the description of the Maltese, were presented to the Emperor Kao-Tsu around 620 CE as a gift from the Holy Roman Emperor in Byzantium. More Maltese were obtained from Muslim traders, making it likely that many Chinese toy dogs go back to those imports.

The Lion or Fu Dog

Prior to the first century, Confucianism and Taoism were the prevailing religions in China. In 61 CE, Emperor Han Ming-Di (28–75) was converted to Buddhism by missionaries he had summoned from India after a dream. As Buddhism spread throughout China, people got their first notion of the lion, a predominant symbol of the new religion. The lion was Buddha's vehicle; it could become large and fill the sky, and Buddha rode on its back if he wished to travel. He could also conveniently cause it to shrink to such smallness that he could carry it in the sleeve of his robe.

As there were no lions in China, and the few sent to the Emperor from the West did not survive, there was no living model of the animal. Then one day someone made the startling discovery that the lion resembled the Emperor's own "Fu Dogs." From then on, these palace dogs were known as "lion dogs," and they are most likely the ancestors of today's Pekingese.

The resemblance between the lion and the Pekingese grew as temple breeders cultivated the appearance of the lion. Statues of the Fu Dogs soon became the protectors of sacred buildings and defenders of the law. It was not uncommon to see these statues, which had mischievous, almost devilish faces, guarding tombs or placed in front of government buildings to scare evil spirits.

None other than Marco Polo commented on the lions that lived briefly in the menagerie of Kublai Khan, who conquered all of China in the late 1200s. Polo, who had seen lions in his travels, said, "These beasts were small and short of body. They are astonishingly like the golden-coated nimble dogs which the people bred in their homes."

Pekingese in the Lap of Luxury

In the Chinese capital of Peking (now known as Beijing), emperors raised the little dogs almost to a height of religious veneration, secluding them from the Western world behind a veil of mystery. Favorite dogs were given ranks, such as dukes and princes, and were granted revenues. Female dogs became duchesses and princesses. Imperial guards kept watch over them, and personal servants took them for exercise, gave them daily baths, sprinkled them with fragrant perfumes, and laid them to nap on silken cushions. Special meals were prepared, and they were fed from porcelain plates.

It was custom for the emperor to select four Pekingese to become his bodyguards. These four dogs would precede the emperor on occasions of state, two of them announcing his approach at correct intervals with sharp, piecing barks, the other two daintily holding the hem of his royal robe in their mouths. At night they carried little lanterns strapped to their necks. The dogs were famed for their vigilance and would bark a sharp warning if danger approached.

The highly prized 4- to 5-pound (1.5 to 2 kg) sleeve-dogs were carried in the huge sleeves of the long robes worn by the royals, startling adversaries with their ferocious temperament. Small size and distinctive markings were the highest valued traits.

Taking royal dogs of any breed from the precincts of the palace was considered a crime worthy of death or other Chinese tortures. It was not until 1905 that the Empress Cixi (see sidebar) abolished this form of punishment.

Amazingly, during these many centuries, regardless of who seized the throne, native or foreign, the Pekingese remained as the symbol for the emperor or empress's well-being, and he passed his days in safety and reverence under the protection of the mighty monarchs.

Breeding the Pekingese

From around 800 CE, the breeding of toy dogs escalated in China, except for the years 1368–1628. Those emperors worshipped cats and kept thousands of them in the palace. The cats had official ranks and titles and were fed by servants of the emperor.

During the Manchurian rule, from 1644–1911, Pekingese and other dogs came back as the revered animal of choice. Within the confines of the Imperial

THE EMPRESS CIXI

Cixi is the Pinyin name for the Empress. (Pinyin is a system used to spell Chinese names in foreign publications.) In older texts using the Latin alphabet to write Chinese, she is known as Empress Tz'u-hsi.

Palace, eunuchs by the thousands were assigned the task of breeding and caring for the dogs. Imperial Dog Books, which were strictly guarded, were used as the standard means of record keeping. These scrolls were illustrated with depictions of the most prized Fu dogs, thought to be models for the breeders. The highest compliment a breeder could be given was to have a specimen good enough to go into this Imperial Book. Very few of these books have been allowed to leave the palaces, but those that have been obtained portray dogs closely resembling the Pekingese, the Pug, and the Shih Tzu.

The eunuchs vied with each other to win royal favor, experimenting in hopes of producing unusual colors or features. Sadly, cruel measures were used to create the desired facial expression and diminutive size.

In the 17th century, the palaces and monasteries of China and Tibet began to exchange dogs. Pekingese were crossed with other dogs known at that time: rough- and smooth-coated Pugs, Japanese Chin, Tibetan Spaniels, Lhasa Apsos, Tibetan Terriers, and Chow Chows. The cross between the Pekingese and the Lhasa Apso eventually became what we know today as the Shih Tzu.

In the 19th century or earlier, Pekingese were produced in rough and smooth coat varieties, with the latter known as "Happa (under the table) Dogs." The smooths apparently were bred out of the gene pool soon after the turn of the 20th century. Ta-Jen, a "unique little Happa dog," was the only one known in England. He was bought by the Hon. Mrs. Lancelot Carnegie while part of a delegation to Peking, a designation that no doubt helped her acquire the dog.

The Dowager Empress Cixi

In the mid-1800s, during the rule of Dowager Empress Cixi (1835–1908), dogs were bred to resemble lions to the utmost. The Empress demanded that the coats were made to be golden and more feathered, and their muzzles were to be made wider. The Imperial kennel, which had perhaps thousands of dogs, was subject to periodic review by the Empress. If she wished to examine one of the dogs more closely, one of the eunuchs would hold the dog up for her examination. If she did not approve of the dog, it was taken away. What became of these rejected dogs no one knows for sure, but occasionally the dogs would show up on the black market or in the homes of commoners.

The Empress preferred Pekingese of brighter shades to go with her imperial costumes. Apparently she did not like the white dogs, as white is the Chinese color of mourning. To her credit, the Empress did stop the cruel methods used by the eunuchs to stunt growth and shorten noses. She preferred to produce certain traits by judicious breeding. As an artist, she enjoyed painting the dogs. Oddly, unlike her predecessors, the Empress was rarely seen holding the dogs or spending time with them, and she always washed her hands after holding one. The little dogs were devoted to her, though, and listened for her step and her voice.

The Second Opium War

When French and British troops stormed the Imperial Palace in 1860, much of the royal family had already fled. The Empress had left behind many treasures, including a number of Pekingese. Some of

Pekingese were dogs of Chinese royalty for centuries.

the dogs ended up in the hands of street merchants, some with commoners, some as ship mascots, and some were taken away by the soldiers. Sadly, many had been destroyed by order of the Empress to prevent them from "falling into the profane hands of barbarians."

During this invasion, British soldiers made an incredible discovery in one of the Imperial apartments. They found the body of the Emperor's aunt, who had committed suicide to avoid capture. Guarding her body were five little Pekingese. Whether they put up a struggle when captured, no one will ever know, but these five dogs made their way to England. In 1861, the most famous of these dogs (appropriately named Lootie) was presented to Queen Victoria, with whom Lootie lived until she died in 1872. Not many dogs can claim to have lived with two of the most powerful women in the world!

Had those five dogs and perhaps a few of their companions not been seized, the breed very well could have become extinct. Unfortunately, the only two of those five who were bred were those presented to the Duke and Duchess of Richmond and Gordon.

The Empress returned in 1861 to reestablish civil order, but many of her Pekingese and other royal dogs had already been dispersed. However, she did much to improve the breeding program of those who remained. She delighted in breeding special patterns and colors that had links with the symbols of Buddhism. The white blaze upon the forehead, for example, was highly prized as "a superior mark of Buddha," which the Chinese called "a little ball shining like snow between the eyebrows."

The Boxer Rebellion

The Empress's plotting against the Western powers nearly brought her reign to an end during the Boxer Rebellion in 1900. Once more she was forced to flee, only to return a mellower ruler. She made more contact with foreigners and presented some of her dogs as gifts to foreign dignitaries, including Miss Alice Roosevelt, the daughter of Theodore Roosevelt. She even allowed an American artist, Miss Carl, to paint her portrait, and then presented her with a parti-colored Pekingese.

In 1908 Empress Cixi died after suffering a stroke. Her funeral procession was led through the countryside for four days. Moo-Tan, a yellow-and-white dog with a white spot on his forehead, was led before her coffin by the chief eunuch following the precedent that had been set nine hundred years before, when the favorite dog of the Emperor T'ai Tsung of the Sung Dynasty was led in state to his master's tomb. No doubt an effigy of the dog was placed in Cixi's tomb to accompany her to her afterlife.

THE PEKINGESE PERSONALITY

"Decidedly different from any other breed—or any other living thing, for that matter—the Pekingese has changed little since the days of his murky origin. He retains the imperial attitude he lorded around the palace, and his presence in his household is not commensurate with his size. His make and shape remain the same as they did then, from the tip of the tail held defiantly or triumphantly way up over his back to the large dark eyes which miss nothing but ignore much. Even at his tiniest—known as a Sleeve, for that's where he was carried in the robes of the palace dwellers—he is fearlessly, fiercely loyal to his people, possessions, and goals. And yet he can be more than a bit of a clown and will delight his family with all sorts of antics, odd characteristics, and qualities. A Pekingese never forgets; this can be good, if he's remembering a friend, and bad when he reconnects with a foe. He is independent and enjoys his own time table; if you're lucky you occupy a large part. Off on his own he is never, ever bored, but no dog makes a better bed or lap companion than he, if and when he wants. If there is a drawback to the Pekingese temperament, it is that he is very reluctant to acknowledge minor aches and pains, so problems can progress without your knowledge, until they can no longer be ignored. No prissy little dog, the Pekingese. He's a large dog in a little body and he's big enough to fill up our entire heart."

—Joseph Neil McGinnis, breeder/owner/handler of The ElphaSun
Pekingese, Register of Merit, All Breed Best in Show and
Specialty Best in Show winners, and Publisher of
The Orient Express, the world's longest-running Pekingese publication

The Pekingese Comes West

In 1893 a gray brindle, apparently stolen from the Imperial Palace, was smuggled to a Captain Loftus Allen, master of a trading ship. "Peking Peter" had the honor of being the first Pekingese ever exhibited. Mrs. Loftus Allen showed him in 1894 in the foreign class at the Chester dog show in England. Captain Allen would later "obtain" two more specimens, and more would follow from other sources, legitimately or not.

In 1898 the English Kennel Club recognized the breed as the Pekingese Spaniel, enabling it to compete for championships. The first English champion was Champion Goodwood Lo. By 1904 the popularity of the breed dictated that it was time for a club to be formed solely for Pekingese, and the British Pekingese Club was founded.

The Pekingese in America

In the early 1900s the Pekingese was becoming the rage in America. The sophisticated image of this palace dog appealed in particular to the affluent members of society.

The American Kennel Club (AKC) recognized the breed in 1906, and the first AKC champion (in 1907) was Tsang of Downshire, an English import and grandson of one of the "looted" dogs obtained by the Duke and Duchess of Richmond and Gordon. Tsang proved to be a very important Pekingese in future pedigrees.

Empress Cixi gave several palace dogs to Americans as gifts. A black Pekingese named Chaou Ching U' was given to Dr. Mary H. Cotton, and the dog became the first female American champion.

In the non-show world, from the 1910s to the early 1930s, the Peke's paw prints could be seen all over the glamorous worlds of design and fashion. In a 1917 issue of *Vogue*, humorist Dorothy Parker said, "No woman who owns that lily of the field, a Pekingese, can be accused of selfishness; she simply hasn't the time to think of herself. His Serene Highness demands unceasing attention." Novelist

The Pekingese Club of America was formed in 1909.

TIMELINE

- **61 CE:** Buddhism comes to China, and Buddha's lion becomes an important part of the culture.
- **620 CE:** Two Maltese are presented to Emperor Kou Tzu as a gift from the Holy Roman Emperor.
- **800 CE:** Breeding smaller dogs escalates in China, using Maltese and native temple dogs.
- **Mid-1800s:** Palace eunuchs strive to breed dogs to look like lions to please the Empress Cixi.
- **1860:** Foreign troops storm the Imperial Palace and the Empress leaves behind a number of Pekingese.
- **1861:** One of the Imperial Palace Pekingese, Lootie, is presented to Queen Victoria.
- **1898:** The English Kennel Club recognizes the breed as the Pekingese Spaniel, enabling it to compete for championships.
- **1901:** A Pekingese named Pekin is the first to be shown in the United States.
- **1909:** The Pekingese Club of America is founded.

Edith Wharton would own several Pekes in the 1920s. Tallulah Bankhead starred in the theatre production of Jacque Deval's *The Cardboard Lover* with the first of her many Pekes, Napoleon.

One very lucky Pekingese, Sun Yat Sen, owned by Henry Harper of the New York publishing firm Harper & Row, was one of three dogs to survive the Titanic. (The other two were Pomeranians.) On the night of the tragedy, April 15, 1912, Henry and his wife, Myra, were having dinner. They were then told to go back to their cabin, dress warmly, put on their lifebelts, and go up to the boat deck. Henry put on an overcoat over his dinner tuxedo, and Myra put on a black fur coat over her sparkly dinner dress. They then ventured out onto the starboard side and boarded Lifeboat 3, carrying Sun Yat Sen. The occupants of Lifeboat 3 were rescued by the Carpathia at around 6 a.m. on April 15. When asked later about the dog being brought onto a lifeboat, Henry stated,

"There seemed to be lots of room and nobody made any objection."

The Pekingese Club of America

The Pekingese Club of America (PCA) was formed in 1909 with Dr. Mary Cotton among its founders. The club's early patrons included Lady Algernon Gordon Lennox, a breed pioneer and visionary in the United Kingdom, and famed financier John Pierpont Morgan, who became the club's Honorary President as well as Vice Chairman of the Peking Palace Dog Association in Britain. Mrs. Morgan could frequently be seen in public with her Peke, Pou Sa.

The club's inaugural specialty show was a huge society event held in 1911, in the ballroom of Manhattan's Plaza Hotel. According to the *New York Times*, the show "attracted scores of society folks." Dog pens were decorated with elaborate embroidery work, no doubt beautiful Chinese embroidery. The judge was one of the club's founders, Mrs. Benjamin (Bridget) Guinness, who wore long white gloves and sat on a chair while all the dogs were brought to her, one at a time. Her breed winner was Tsang of Downshire. The Empress Cixi offered a silver cup as a trophy. As extravagant as this may seem, it was, after all, a fitting tribute to a dog who was a member of China's royal family.

The PCA now has more than 350 members throughout the world. It is dedicated to responsible dog ownership and advocates for the Pekingese dog as a family companion and show dog. It protects and advances Pekingese health and well-being and works to educate Pekingese breeders, owners, judges, and the public about the proper care and distinctiveness of the Pekingese.

PCA annual national specialties are now held at various locations around the country.

The Pekingese Today

The Pekingese no longer rules the imperial courts of China and more likely carries a squeaky toy rather than the hem of an emperor's robe. In fact, he has downsized quite a bit, feeling as much at home in an apartment as he did in a palace. Although ranked somewhere in the middle of AKC registrations, you wouldn't know it by the way he walks, head thrown back, nose in the air, ears softly swaying, with that air of royalty.

Chapter
2

Characteristics of the Pekingese

A breed standard is written by breed clubs and approved by the American Kennel Club (AKC) in order to give breeders and judges guidelines to determine which dogs are most suitable for breeding stock. Standards define a breed in terms of size, coat, color, head type, temperament— what makes them distinctive from any other breed. Of course, no dog is perfect, not even the greatest of champions!

The complete Pekingese Club of America (PCA) standard can be found on the club website at www. thepekingeseclubofamerica.com.

The Pekingese Look

The Empress Cixi is credited with writing the original breed standard for the Pekingese. While there is not enough room to print her entire standard here, some of it will be highlighted to show how poetically she describes her beloved breed.

Size

Empress Cixi: Let the Lion Dog be small; let it wear the swelling cape of dignity around its neck; let it display the billowing standard of pomp above its back.

Modern Pekingese generally are larger than those who lived in the Imperial Palace. Pekes weigh from 7 to 14 pounds (3 to 6 kg) and stand about 6 to 9 inches (15 to 23 cm) at the withers (shoulder) but can be smaller. These smaller Pekes are commonly referred to as "Sleeve" Pekingese or just "Sleeves," from when emperors carried the smallest ones in their sleeves. The PCA has a disqualification for dogs over 14 pounds (6 kg).

The wrinkle is one of the most recognizable characteristics of the Pekingese.

Check It Out

PEKE FAST FACTS

✓ The first Pekingese breed standard was written by Chinese Empress Cixi.

✓ Pekingese are not generally athletic, but some have excelled in companion events.

✓ Pekingese get along with well-mannered children, dogs, and cats under most circumstances.

✓ Pekes are as happy in a small apartment as in an Imperial Palace but still need moderate exercise.

✓ Due to their structure, Pekes should avoid hot weather and situations where their breathing is stressed.

✓ Some people perceive the Peke's stubbornness as lack of intelligence, but they are actually quite smart.

✓ Pekes do not always learn things as quickly as some other breeds, but once they learn it, they are more reliable.

The Pekingese is unexpectedly heavy for his size, with a stocky, muscular body that should be pear shaped, compact, and low to the ground. Pekes are actually lighter in the rear than in the front, somewhat of a surprise when you pick one up. The head is large in proportion to the body. The Peke is slightly longer than tall.

Coat

Empress Cixi's "cape of dignity" refers to the noticeable mane on the neck and shoulder area. The coat on the remainder of the body, which is somewhat shorter in length, is a long, coarse-textured, straight, stand-off outer coat, with a thick, soft undercoat. A long and profuse coat is acceptable as long as it does not obscure the natural outline of the dog.

Head

Empress Cixi: Let its face be black; let its forefront be shaggy; let its forehead be straight and low, Like unto the brow of an Imperial harmony boxer.

The current standard (approved in 2004) calls for a black mask or a self-colored face (self-mask). This means that the mask can be some other color present on the dog, or there may not be a mask at all. Regardless of coat color, the exposed skin of the muzzle, nose, lips, and eye rims should be black. An earlier breed standard stated that a black mask and spectacles around the eyes with lines to the ears is a desirable trait. This marking makes a beautiful Pekingese face.

The Empress's reference to the "Imperial harmony boxer" is less clear. She supported the Society of Righteous and Harmonious Fists (boxers) in the Boxer Rebellion in 1900, but how the brow (or wrinkle?) of our Pekingese compares to those of the members of this secret society is unclear, at least to your author!

The Wrinkle

Empress Cixi: The wrinkle is one of the most recognizable characteristics of the Pekingese.

First, picture the face from the front. The top skull is massive, broad and flat, and wider than deep (from front to back) to create a rectangular-shaped head. The eyes are wide-set and forward-looking. In profile, the face is flat with the chin, nose, and brow lying in one plane, slanting very slightly backward. (This will be much easier to picture if you are looking at an actual dog!)

The wrinkle separates the upper and lower areas of the face. It is a hair-covered fold of skin extending from one cheek over the bridge of the nose in a wide inverted V to the other cheek. It is important that the wrinkle not be too large, especially if it interferes with the eyes. If too large and round, this is known to breeders as a "sausage wrinkle."

Muzzle and Mouth

The muzzle should be very flat and broad. The skin should be black, but light-colored Pekes often have lighter skin.

Whiskers add to the desired expression. The lower jaw is broad and undershot, meaning the lower jaw protrudes farther than the upper jaw, and the front teeth do not meet. The black lips should meet neatly, and the teeth and tongue should not show when the mouth is closed.

Eyes, Ears, and Nose

Empress Cixi: Let its eyes be large and luminous; let its ears be set like the sails of war junk; let its nose be like that of the monkey god of the Hindus.

The eyes should be large, very dark, round, lustrous, and set wide apart, and should not bulge. The eye rims are black, and the white of the eye should not show when the dog is looking straight ahead. The Chinese believed that if too much white showed, it meant bad-tempered (though there is no scientific evidence for that!).

The ears are endearingly heart-shaped, lie flat against the head, and do not extend below the jaw. With their heavy feathering and long fringing, the ears should frame the sides of the face and add to the appearance of a wide, rectangular head. Perhaps the Empress intended for the Pekingese ears to be efficient like the sails of her nation's sailing vessels (junks), the sails of which can be moved inward, toward the long axis of the ship, allowing it to sail into the wind.

As for the nose, it should be broad, short, and black with nostrils that are wide and open rather than pinched. The more pinched the nostrils are, the more likely the Peke will have breathing problems, especially in the heat. We know from the fable in Chapter 1 that the Pekingese is "part monkey," hence the resemblance of its nose to the monkey god of the Hindus!

This is a good opportunity to bring up another well-known trait of the Pekingese. With his short face, he is a master of the four S's: snorting, snuffling, sneezing, and snoring. And this is pretty much a given!

Body, Legs, and Gait

Empress Cixi: Let its forelegs be bent; so that it shall not desire to wander far, or leave the Imperial precincts... Let its feet be tufted with plentiful hair that its footfall may be soundless and for its standard of pomp let it rival the whick (perhaps tail hair) *of the Tibetans' yak, which is flourished to protect the imperial litter from flying insects.*

The bones of the forelegs should be moderately bowed, even though some ancient paintings showed the dogs with straight legs. The gait is unhurried, dignified, free and strong, with a slight roll over the shoulders. The motion should be smooth and effortless and as free as possible from bouncing, prancing or jarring. The front feet are turned out slightly when standing or moving, much as with the true lion.

The Pekingese has a stocky, muscular body that should be pear shaped, compact, and low to the ground.

The long furnishings on the toes are referred to as slippers. While the breed standard calls for no trimming for the show ring, slippers are trimmed to some degree so that they don't trip the dog and impede walking.

There should also be feathering on the backs of the thighs and forelegs, as well as longer fringing on the ears and tail. The topline (outline of dog from shoulders to tail) should be straight. The dog should not look as if he is going down steps.

The tail, which is an important part of the dog's outline, should be slightly arched and carried well over the back, free of kinks or curls. (Some Asian dog breed standards allow the dog's tail to be tightly curled toward the back of the dog.) The tail should have long, profuse, straight fringing that may fall to either side. The modern-day Pekingese tail may or may not be able to protect the litter from flying insects!

Color

Empress Cixi: And for its colour, let it be that of the lion—a golden sable, to be carried in the sleeve of a yellow robe; or the colour of a red bear, or a black and white bear, or striped like a dragon, so that there may be dogs appropriate to every costume in the Imperial wardrobe.

Pekes may have any coat color and markings, as per the PCA standard. The majority are gold, red, or sable. The Empress was said to have dogs bred to match the flowers in her garden as well as to match her robes. The rarest dogs matched her chrysanthemums—pale yellow and white. Pure white Pekingese were not popular, since they were regarded as the embodiment of the spirit of some great man now deceased. But not to worry! There are many white Pekingese who do very well as show dogs and as pets. These white Pekes are not to

The Peke's majestic history and unique personality make him a valued addition to the family.

be confused with albino Pekes. Albinos cannot be shown and can have serious health concerns.

Temperament

Empress Cixi: Let it be lively that it may afford entertainment by its gambols (antics); let it be timid that it may not involve itself in danger… Let it comport itself with dignity; let it learn to bite the foreign devils instantly. Thus shall it preserve its integrity and self-respect… So shall it remain—but if it dies, remember thou too art mortal.

The AKC standard requires that the Pekingese temperament be one of directness, independence, and individuality. Its image is lionlike, implying courage, dignity, boldness, and self-esteem rather than daintiness or delicacy.

To paraphrase someone owned and loved by a Peke, he may growl to show his self-importance. He may defend his territory, even if the "enemy" is three times his size. He may also defend his human. But the growling is all show. Inside, the little dogs have a heart of gold. Once a Peke trusts you, he will become a loyal friend for life.

Occasionally a Peke will be too aggressive as a watchdog and will stand his ground to get noticed. However, aggression is not the norm. Your Peke should never growl at you in an aggressive manner. Distinctive temperaments are

Ask the Expert

LOVE AND DEVOTION

"**P**ekingese are lovers. They do things for you because they love you. Once they know you care, they will give you more love than you can ever give them. They are very devoted. They are fearless like a lion. Some like to be cuddled, some just like to be at your feet and look up at you with those big eyes. Pekes are absolutely marvelous!"

—Arlon D. Duit, Lon-Du Pekingese, breeder and exhibitor since 1976

based on the quality of the breeding and how they were socialized. This is the case in any breed of dog.

Living With the Pekingese

The Pekingese is a very popular family pet, especially with single families, those with older children, and seniors. His majestic history and unique personality make him a valued addition to the family.

Personality

The Pekingese takes great pride in his possessions, from his toys to his bed, which, of course, should be made only of the most lavish materials. He is not likely to tear anything up, not even the errant slipper.

Some Pekes are offended when treated like mere dogs. Those Pekes would rather stick their noses in the air and be admired from a respectable distance. Yet one of those same dogs might surprise you with sudden appeals for attention.

A Pekingese normally does not bark as much as other toys, which makes him

a good candidate for apartment living or traveling to hotels. He will notify you, though, if something is suspicious.

The Peke is courageous, loyal, and protective toward his humans. He is not likely to start a fight, but with his "lion heart" he will be quick to protect his family, even though he may think he is larger and braver than he really is. He is seldom flustered by the unexpected and takes everything in stride.

Although he is much heavier than most other toy breeds, he can be carried when necessary. Being a lapdog would normally not be his preference, but he will comply if it makes you happy. He may even nudge you from time to time to let you know he is there if you need him. He may get too warm sitting in your lap, so if he wants to leave, be sure to let him. Like many of us, he likes air conditioning and really appreciates an ice pack in his bed if the house is warm.

Don't let him jump off furniture, as he could hurt his back. Ramps or little steps can help him navigate to his favorite spot.

He is a stubborn breed. When it comes to training, this can be frustrating. Some people perceive this trait as lack of intelligence. This is not the case at all. He simply needs to know why you threw that toy in the first place if you only want it back. You, as trainer, need to let him know there is a purpose in all of this.

The Peke does not learn by repetition. That is boring to someone of such refinement. His stubbornness can pay off, though, in sickness or in pain. He has a strong will to live and a strong endurance for pain.

Yet the breed is not for everyone. He generally is not an athletic dog. He cannot be handled roughly in play, as he may become irritated or even injured. He can be very sensitive, and he resents being scolded. However, if he respects you, he will be well mannered. In return, he will want respect from you and will do whatever it takes to get it.

Companionability

A Pekingese can be a delightful companion for a well-mannered child, but may not be athletic or playful enough for some children. Most importantly, children need to understand that a dog is a living thing and deserves respect. In play, the child may unintentionally poke or startle the puppy or adult dog. Teach the child to approach the dog calmly and speak softly. And do not leave them unattended until you are sure both will be safe together.

It is important to teach the child the dangers of touching the Peke's eyes or hampering his breathing. Once these boundaries are established, the Peke can be a very good dog for a child. As the child gets older, she can learn about the magical history behind this charming dog—and may even get involved in showing or other activities.

Pekingese are generally quite capable of sharing the house with a cat or with another dog. Introduce them gradually, perhaps on neutral territory. The new friends should not be left alone until you are sure they will get along. Both animals need a safe spot where they can go to be away from each other as needed. If there's a possibility that your cat's claws may

Teach your child the appropriate way to handle a Pekingese.

Puppy Love

PUPS WITH AN ATTITUDE

Pekingese have a natural "attitude." As one fancier said, "They are born with the delusion that they own the world, and their lifelong goal is to convince everyone else that this is indeed true." This is quite possibly the trait that attracted you to the breed to begin with, so you certainly will not want to curtail it. You will want him to behave, however, and this should begin in puppyhood.

come in contact with the dog, be careful about the Peke's eyes during play time!

Being a large lion in a small dog's body, the Pekingese may get a little overconfident with larger, aggressive dogs and try to fight. This "small dog syndrome" is common with many toy breeds. It may be necessary to feed both dogs separately and crate them while you are gone. A Pekingese can sustain serious damages from a fight.

If you already have a dog and are considering a second one, it is best to choose one of the opposite sex. Dogs of the same sex are more likely to fight, and most males tend to be submissive to females. If you do choose two dogs of the same sex, two males are more likely to coexist than two females. Females tend to try for the alpha position in the pack, possibly leading to fighting. And many people report that it is much harder to break up two females than two males. This is not to say that the Pekingese is a breed known to fight—it certainly is not.

However, anything can happen when hormones are involved.

Environment

A Pekingese can be happy anywhere, from a small apartment to a luxurious estate. He is quite content snoozing on his plush pillow while the family goes about their daily activities. He also enjoys going on new adventures by car or by chariot— that is, his stroller. A Peke will delight in a nice walk, observing his kingdom and lapping up any attention he can get from his subjects.

A large yard is not necessary, but some Pekes do enjoy playing outside. He should never be left outside alone under any circumstances. There are dangers lurking in a yard that may not be issues with other breeds. If a Peke tries to dig or sniff a foreign object, it may injure his nasal passages or even his eyes. And if it should get too warm outside, it could be dangerous for him.

Brachycephalic, or short-faced dogs,

PEKINGESE AND CHILDREN

A Pekingese can be a delightful companion for a well-mannered child. The dog's slow pace, gentle demeanor, and big heart can provide a child with the most wonderful childhood experience. Supervise the twosome until you are sure the child is mature enough to understand how to properly carry, pet, and play with the Peke. Above all, teach the child to respect the unique physical structure of the breed—the eyes, the breathing, etc.—for the safety of both of them.

have a high risk of heatstroke because they can't pant vigorously enough to lower their body heat. Keep him away from allergenic pollen and freshly cut grass or anything that is sprayed that he may inhale.

Exercise Requirements

The regal Pekingese doesn't require much exercise, but he will stay in better health if he has regular opportunities to run around and play. Just be sure he does so within the confines of the weather, and always be vigilant about his exercise tolerance. The Peke is more rugged than most toy breeds, but when overexercised he can have difficulty breathing. Make sure he is free to move around in case he gets too warm.

Many Pekes have made it in the world of athletics in obedience, rally, and agility. Sports are definitely not off limits for this breed.

In hot or humid weather, minimize his outdoor activity or keep him in an air-conditioned house.

For his safety, walk him using a Y-shaped harness that wraps around his chest, not his throat. A collar puts pressure on his windpipe and makes it harder for him to breathe. (See Chapter 3 for more information on harnesses.)

Grooming

A Pekingese requires a great deal of grooming. The thick coat needs to be brushed regularly, and the eyes must be checked daily for any sign of inflammation, dryness, or irritation. The wrinkle must be kept clean and dry. Your Peke's breeder may have started training your puppy to be groomed from an early age. If not, this is a priority when he first joins your household. This extensive grooming is something you should consider before adding a Pekingese to your family.

Trainability

Unlike many breeds of dogs that aim to please their owners, the Pekingese will do what you ask only if he feels it is in his best interest. Most Peke parents find this personality an endearing trait! However, before that endearing trait becomes a problem, a little training may be in order. We'll go into specifics in Chapter 6, but for now, some basics.

Some dogs seem to learn by repetition, but repetition will bore a Pekingese. If he is going to comply, he will do so within the first few attempts. If he doesn't, stop. Move on to another exercise. It just won't happen! He doesn't have to learn everything right away. Take it slowly and take the time to build a connection.

Pekes do not learn things as quickly as some other breeds, but once they learn it, they are more reliable. You may have to be creative in order to outsmart your pupil. Even if it turns out he's not cut out for obedience, you will have spent quality time with him, which is a good thing.

Some Peke parents claim that the little dogs are difficult to housetrain. This appears to be the case with many other toy breeds, maybe in part because the parents let a toy get away with behavior they'd never tolerate in a large dog. A "little pee pee" from a puppy may be cute to the human observers, enough to even encourage the puppy to continue. Or it may be so small in the house it is never noticed. That "little pee pee" will eventually become larger and the parents will become weary of cleaning it up. Or the parents may be reluctant to put such a cute little puppy in a crate for crate training. He is still a D-O-G and needs to be treated as such in these circumstances. (But don't tell him that!)

It is definitely possible to housetrain a Pekingese (or any other toy)—you simply must use the same method you would use for any large dog. Be consistent with your praise and no-no's. Pekingese have long life expectancies, living 12 to 16 years or more, so taking the time to train and modify your Peke's behavior will pay off with years of living with a well-mannered companion.

If you are looking for a smart dog—not a dog trainable by repetition and drills, but a clever, thinking dog—the Pekingese may be for you!

Your Peke doesn't require much exercise but still needs opportunities to run and play.

Chapter
3

Supplies for Your Pekingese

The American Pet Products Association (APPA) estimated that more than $50 billion would be spent on pets in the United States this year. This includes $11 billion on supplies alone. After all, our pets need these things! They need faux mink coats, designer jackets, holiday outfits, and collars and leashes dangling with jewelry. Their sweaters need to be monogrammed. And your Peke must have every toy known to mankind. But seriously, before you bring your new Peke home, there are a few supplies you need to have on hand for his well-being—and enjoyment!

Let's start out with the basics.

Bringing Your Peke Home

A collar and leash (or harness) are must haves for your dog.

Collar and Leash

Take a collar and leash with you when you go to pick up your dog, even if he is not leash trained, just in case he would try to get away. Nylon collars are best for coated breeds, as they cause the least damage to the coat. A little harder to find but even better are the rolled nylon collars for minimal coat damage. You can find very nice matching nylon leashes at 4 feet or 6 feet (1 or 2 m) in length. Extendable leashes, which don't give you

Before you bring your Peke home, you'll need to have some supplies on hand, like a bed.

Puppy Love

SHOPPING LIST FOR YOUR NEW PUPPY

- Puppy food
- Bowls for food and water
- Collar and leash, preferably with ID tags
- Crate for potty training
- Baby gate(s)
- Small, easy to wash bed
- Lots of toys
- Lots of patience!

much control over larger dogs, work fine for the slower-moving Pekingese.

Training collars are recommended only for the obedience ring, especially with the Peke because of the potential for tracheal and eye injuries. Pinch or prong collars should never be used.

Harness

Harnesses give you a safe and secure way to walk your Peke, and they put less strain on the neck and distribute the tension. Make sure the harness fits correctly and does not chafe under the front legs. "No pull" harnesses reduce neck strain by tightening slightly around your dog's chest to discourage pulling. You can even find step-in harnesses, which may be the easiest to use. With the Peke's tendency toward tracheal injuries and eye trauma, a harness may be your best option.

When buying a harness, consider that your dog may have a lot of coat. Snaps or buckles might work better than Velcro, which could catch the hair.

Most importantly, never leave the harness on your Peke when he is lounging at home. Doing this will cause a nightmare of tangles and skin irritations! The skin needs to breathe. If at all possible, leave his collar off at home as well. Collars can catch on something and trap the dog, a dangerous predicament.

Feeding Time for Your Peke

Your Peke has to eat! Here are some items you'll need to keep him well fed.

Food

Your Peke may be bringing along some food from his breeder (or rescue organization), so he can stay on his same diet, at least for a while. Just to make sure, call ahead and find out about his food so that you can have some on hand.

Bowls

Once he gets home, your Peke will need bowls. You can buy stainless steel, glass, and ceramic—there are all kinds of

BEDS

Q: What type of bed do you recommend for your Pekes?

A: "The beds I like best are the cot-type elevated beds that have legs and are a few inches (cm) above the floor. These beds allow the circulation of air and prevent the dog from getting too hot. When I have used cushions the dog eventually gets hot and pushes them aside or ends up lying in the floor. The dogs seem to really like the elevated beds."

—Christine Smith, Maplewood Pekingese

choices. Check to make sure there is no lead-based paint if the bowl is painted. Some dogs are allergic to plastic bowls, and some experts feel the plastic can harbor bacteria, so why take the risk? Bowls that come on stands, however fancy, may be too high for your Peke.

Placemat
Regardless of your choice of bowl, a doggy placemat will help lessen some spills and protect your floor, and there are a lot of cute choices available.

Water
Your Peke should have access to fresh clean water at all times. A pet water bottle is an option if your dog tends to be messy with his water bowl. The bottle can be hung on the inside of his crate. There are also freestanding holders for water bottles. If you decide to use a bottle, make sure he is able to get enough to drink.

Your Peke's Kingdom
Your Peke's ancestors may have had the run of the Imperial Palace, but that may not be what you have in mind for your Peke, at least at first. Any dog needs to know what his boundaries are and where he needs to go to relieve himself.

Baby Gates
Baby gates are the best way to keep your Peke confined until you are sure he is housetrained. You will also want to keep him out of any room that is not dog-proofed and away from any room that has an outside door that could be accidentally left open. You can find accordion-type gates or the type that swing open, both of which need to be screwed into the wall. Spring tension gates are designed to fit various doorway widths and can be taken down easily. Some companies make custom gates out of wood or wrought iron.

A clever way to protect your dog from running out the door, if you don't mind a little inconvenience, is to install a gate between your door and screen door so that he will be barricaded if you need to open the door to receive a package or a pizza.

Doggy Door

Doggy doors provide a way for your pet to go outside to potty, as long as the yard is secured.

Bells

Training bells that hang from your doorknob allow your puppy to alert you that he has to go out with the swat of a paw or the nudge of a nose.

Fencing

Your Peke may be content to stay inside all the time, but there are times when he needs to go outside. Be sure to check your fence perimeter for holes or gaps in the fence, and make sure the gate will latch safely. If you are unable to see the gate from your door, you may want to invest in a lock so that no one will leave it open.

Spot Remover

Yellow lawn spot removers are sold at many lawn and garden stores in case urine damages your grass. If you use a commercial lawn service, check with the company to make sure it doesn't use any chemicals that could harm your pets.

An exercise pen (ex-pen) is a good choice if you need to confine your Peke.

Your Peke's Pad

Crates, ex-pens, and comfy beds all provide safe spots for your Peke to rest.

Crate

A crate is a safe place for your Peke if company comes or if service people are in your house. It can also be his private haven—his own "pad," so to speak. Dogs are den animals, and a crate can become his den when he wants some peace and quiet. If you leave the door open, chances are he will go in on his own, just to get away from it all.

If the crate will be used long term, you will want to get one at least twice as large as the grown dog so that there will be room for his water, bed, toys, etc.

Wire or nylon mesh crates give your dog a view of his surroundings. Check wire crates for sharp edges or corners, as Pekes like to rub their faces against things, and edges could cause injuries. Plastic airline-type crates offer him more privacy but may get hot or seem confining. You can even buy nice wood and wicker crates that blend in with household decor! Whatever the material, examine the construction to make sure your Peke's thick coat will not get caught in the wire or door. Place the crate where the family spends time so that he will not feel isolated.

Many people use crates to housetrain their dogs, which will be discussed in Chapter 6. If used properly, a crate is not a form of punishment.

Exercise Pen

An exercise pen (ex-pen) is a good choice if your Peke will be kept confined while you are away, and it will give him plenty of room for his belongings. Ex-pens are made of metal, plastic, or PVC pipes, and come in any number of panels. Some have small doors in one of the panels, and some will require you to lift your dog out. You won't need terribly high panels for a Pekingese.

Car Travel

For travel in the car, consider a canine car seat, a small crate, or an airline dog carrier. It is not safe to hold a dog on your lap in the car, particularly when you are in a seat protected by air bags. If your car has front seat air bags, keep the dog secured in the back seat. For long trips, take along a few ice packs in case your car breaks down and your dog starts getting warm.

Doggy Stroller

For your daily walks, don't forget about doggy strollers with mesh coverings so that your dog can see out and get plenty of air. These strollers are especially welcomed by older or infirm dogs who can no longer go for a walk with you.

Bed

Pekingese often slept at the foot of the emperor and empress's bed to warm their feet. If you feel you don't need a majestic foot warmer, your Peke will need a bed befitting his status.

If hand-carved teak beds and brocaded silk fabrics are not in your budget, you still have an endless choice of dog beds to choose from. Donut beds, sofa beds, water beds, heated beds—even orthopedic beds. Beds that are washable or have washable covers are the best buy. A Peke-sized bed should fit into a standard washing machine. Like a child, your dog may be just as happy in the box the bed came in!

He will love his bed and spend plenty of time there as long as he is able to move around if he gets too warm. Many Peke parents use ice or gel packs in the beds (or crates), especially if the dog needs to be outside. Movement is the key—he must be able to cool off when necessary.

Potty Time for Your Peke

Housetraining aids you may need for your Peke include the following.

Pee Pads

A lot of toy dog parents train puppies to use pee or piddle pads. These pads, which you place on the floor near an outside door, are made of absorbent

Beds that are washable or have washable covers are best.

CLEAN-UP DETAIL

When you decide to buy or adopt a Peke, be aware that you will have to vacuum more often. If the hair on the carpet becomes too dense, use a rubber broom to get the loose hair from your carpet before you vacuum. For hard-to-reach areas, lightly spritz the carpet with water, then don a pair of rubber gloves and gather the hair into clumps for easy pick-up. A slicker brush is good for getting hair off steps, too.

Lint rollers or brushes are a must for the Peke household. Furniture cleaners made with pets in mind can get out dog hairs that are deeply embedded into the fabric.

Frequently brushing your Peke will cut down on the shedding a great deal.

material with a plastic bottom that protects the floor underneath. Some are scented to attract the dog. Ideally, if you can train your dog to go outside most of the time and also use piddle pads, you will have that option in bad weather or when staying somewhere where it is not convenient to take your dog outside.

Indoor Pet Toilet

There are several versions of an indoor pet toilet made of a thick layer of synthetic grass on a square base. Some even have a drainage system. The most discerning Peke will appreciate not having to "go" in public!

Belly Bands and Panties

For males, the belly band wraps around the mid-section, covering the penis. It doesn't always stop a dog from hiking his leg, but it does catch the urine if he does. The liner of the belly band needs to be changed as necessary. If your female is not yet spayed, you can buy little panties to prevent her from staining surfaces when she is in season. Of course, prepare to keep her inside or guarded from neighborhood strays for as long as three weeks.

Cleanup

Enzyme cleaners that claim to modify odor molecules and reduce odor can be used to prevent the pup from going back to the same place. An ultraviolet light will light up areas you may have missed—and it's pretty cool to use!

For cleanup, a long-handled pooper-scooper will keep you from having to bend over so often. When you take your Peke for a walk, carry along some plastic bags. You can buy cute little plastic bags in a roll that fits into a small dispenser that attaches to your belt. Many cities have strict laws about picking up after your dog.

Your Peke's Good Looks

Grooming will be discussed in Chapter 5, but to start out, invest in a good-quality steel pin brush and a wide-tooth steel comb, with or without a handle—whichever feels better in your hand. Pekes typically don't wear topknots or bows the way some other toys do.

It may take a while to find the perfect shampoo for your Peke, as coat texture differs from dog to dog. Start out with a good-quality dog shampoo and cream rinse formulated for a coated breed, preferably a tearless shampoo. Look in the human baby products aisle for foam shampoo to use on the face. Baby wipes are great for daily cleaning.

Clothes Make the Peke... or Do They?

Every designer from Paris Hilton to Ralph Lauren has a line of coats, sweaters, and dresses for your Peke. You can find collars and tags loaded with Swarovski crystals. Does that mean your Peke needs to be dressed up to look like Jack Sparrow or Lady Ga Ga? It depends partly on how you want to spend time with your dog, but most importantly on whether it makes the dog happy. Some dogs thrive on attention from their people no matter how it comes. They love going to boutiques and having strangers make a fuss over them. Others are unhappy even while being fitted for a basic collar.

Find a happy medium. Spend quality time with your Peke, and if it makes him happy to slip on a little T-shirt or some faux fur, what is the harm? Just don't let your Peke get overheated or wear clothing that impedes movement.

If your dog is very young, clipped down, ill, or elderly, a sweater or coat will be much appreciated in cold weather. And you will appreciate a doggy raincoat even more when you return home in rainy weather with a dry dog. Your dog will probably put up a fight if you try boots to keep his feet warm and dry, but sometimes they can be a plus as well.

If your Peke enjoys wearing clothes, just make sure they don't impede his movement or get him overheated.

Your Peke's Playthings

Chances are your Peke will put TOYS at the top of the shopping list, or second only to treats. Knowing Pekes, it might be best to let him choose his own treasures, but you can guide him a little bit. Latex toys are better than vinyl, which can be chewed off in hard chunks. Plush toys are a favorite of many dogs, but monitor the play to make sure he doesn't disembowel the toy at the first play session. If he is a gentle chewer, a plush toy can last for years. Nylabones are recommended for busy chewers and help keep the teeth clean. They are similar to real bones but don't splinter and can be easily cleaned. If your Peke ends up with mountains of toys, consider putting half of them away for a few months so that they won't become unappreciated. Show interest in his toys and entice him to play. If he thinks they are special to you, they will be more special to him.

Keeping Your Peke Safe

Your Peke needs a means of identification in case he gets out.

ID Tags

A pet supply store, a vet's office, or an online service can make a metal ID tag with everything you need to identify your dog. This is as important as any other pet supply, if not more so.

Microchip

During your first visit to the vet, consider getting your Peke a microchip implant. The chip, which is about the size of a grain of rice and can be read by a scanner, is implanted between the shoulder blades. Most veterinarians and

PREPARING FOR YOUR PEKINGESE

- ✓ Find out what type of food your Peke has been eating so that his tummy won't be upset by a change in diet.
- ✓ Make sure your house is dog-proof by checking for cords, harmful household products, etc.
- ✓ Use baby gates to keep your new dog from exploring on his own.

- ✓ Check your yard for escape routes or dangerous obstacles.
- ✓ Have products available to clean up "accidents"—there probably will be a few.
- ✓ Get an ID tag or microchip implant as soon as you can for your peace of mind.

animal shelters will routinely scan any dog turned in as lost. Dog shows and rescue groups often hold microchip clinics where the implants are offered at a reduced cost.

According to the American Kennel Club (AKC), lost pets with microchips are up to 20 times more likely to be returned home. The AKC Companion Animal Recovery (CAR) service is the nation's largest not-for-profit pet identification and 24/7 recovery service provider.

GPS Pet Locator

The AKC and Positioning Animals Worldwide (PAW) offer the Spotlight GPS pet locator. This combines the recovery services of CAR with the tracking services of GPS technology. For more information, visit www.akccar.org.

License

Many cities and counties require that you license your dog. The city or county will issue a tag for the dog's collar, not only to prove he has been registered but also to help in returning him to you. Check out local laws on dog ownership and responsibilities before acquiring your dog.

Window Sticker

Some fire departments and rescue organizations provide stickers to place in your window or door to alert firefighters and other responders to the presence of a pet in your house or apartment. Stickers are also in many pet supply catalogs. This little sticker can be a lifesaver in the case of a fire or other disaster.

Chapter 4

Feeding Your Pekingese

Empress Cixi decreed that her hundreds of Pekingese should be *"dainty in their food… they should be fed sharks' fins and curlews' livers and the breast of quails… and for their drink… the tea that is brewed from the spring buds of the shrub that grows in the province of the Hankow…"*

If your grocer happens to be out of these ingredients, your Pekingese will be forced to eat the diet of a commoner! However, we will do our best to give you the information you need to select the proper substitutes.

The Balanced Diet

Pekingese, like all other dogs, need a well-balanced diet that provides sufficient calories for growth, activity, and cell repair. Major dog food companies make every effort to provide ingredients in a form that can be easily absorbed into the dogs' systems. Additionally, vitamin and mineral supplements in the food must be balanced. Too much of one mineral may interfere with the absorption of another; too little of a mineral may interfere with vitamin use or other mineral use, and so on.

So the key to good nutrition is balance. But how do we achieve this balance for our Pekingese? Fortunately, veterinarians and nutritionists have been working together to develop a wide variety of balanced foods for our dogs.

Commercial Foods

The first commercial food for dogs was introduced in the 1860s by a young entrepreneur named James Spratt, who was in London selling lightning rods. He happened to notice stray dogs being fed scraps thrown onto the pier by sailors. He decided he could do better, and soon afterward began manufacturing Spratt's Patent Meat Fibrine Dog Cakes, a bone-shaped biscuit made of wheat, vegetables, beetroot, and meat. His company soon thrived selling the product to English country gentlemen for their sporting dogs.

Spratt eventually brought his product to the United States, where it became Spratt's Patent Limited. It became one of the most heavily marketed brands in the early 20th century. The company bought the entire front cover of the American Kennel Club (AKC)'s first journal in January 1889 to announce its involvement with American and European kennel clubs. In the 1950s, Spratt's became part of General Mills.

Today the pet owner has an astonishing array of foods to consider, from breed specific to disease specific, canned, bagged, dehydrated, and frozen. Some products are labeled natural or organic and include ingredients said to promote health, such as duck, blueberries, and omega-3 fatty acids. Venison dog food is getting popular because it is high in protein and lacks unhealthy cholesterol.

Check It Out

FEEDING YOUR PEKE

✓ Learn how to read dog food labels.
✓ Compare commercial diets based on content, reviews, and pricing.
✓ Get assistance from a nutritionist if you feed home-cooked or raw diets.

✓ Avoid letting your Peke become obese, as it can actually affect his breathing.
✓ Let family members know what foods can be toxic to your Peke.

Assessing Commercial Diets

Nutritionists determine whether a canine diet is adequate based on food composition. This technique involves separating the food into six factions: moisture, ash, crude protein, ether extract, crude fiber, and nitrogen-free extract. (The way these calculations come about is beyond the scope of this book.) Those nutrients are compared to the amount recommended, usually by the Association of American Feed Control Officials (AAFCO), a regulating body of the pet food industry. These protocols are useful because they provide a way for us to assess the product. You can visit the association's website at www.aafco.org to learn exactly how to evaluate food labels and how much of each nutrient is necessary for a healthy dog.

Fat, Protein, and Carbohydrates

If a diet is not carefully formulated, there could be either a deficiency or excess of certain nutrients that could cause problems in the dog, such as obesity or protein deficiencies. For the mathematically inclined, calories are provided by fat, protein, and carbohydrates.

Fat is important, in part because it contains essential fatty acids that have important roles in cell membranes, the immune system, and the circulatory system. This is what keeps your Peke's skin and coat healthy. The recommended minimum fat content on a dry-matter (DM) basis is 5 percent for adults and 8 percent for growth and reproduction.

Protein provides essential amino acids and nitrogen. The recommended minimum protein content on a dry-matter (DM) basis is 18 percent for adults and 22 percent for growth and reproduction. Egg has the highest biological value, 94. Fish meal and milk are close behind with a value of 92. Beef is around 78 and soybean meal is 67. Meat and bone meal

And commercial foods that contain a great deal of soy can lead to flatulence (passing gas) in your Peke—and you certainly don't want that!

Minerals and Vitamins

Confused? Minerals and vitamins are a little easier to understand. The two most important minerals are calcium and phosphorus. They must be balanced to provide for proper bone growth in young dogs and to maintain metabolic function throughout various stages of life. AAFCO's recommendation for calcium is 0.6 percent DM for adult maintenance and 1.0 percent DM for growth and reproduction. The phosphorus recommendation is currently 0.5 (adults) and 0.8 (growth) percent of DM. Phosphorus is widely available in many food sources, and deficiency is rare. Calcium deficiency is more likely and results in conditions such as rickets and soft bones. An all-meat diet may cause calcium deficiency because meat is rich in phosphorus but low in calcium. This imbalance can lead to abnormal bone metabolism and severe skeletal problems.

Vitamin A is important for vision. A deficiency of vitamin A can cause dry eye, which is a problem in the Pekingese. But an excess of vitamin A can cause retarded growth, anorexia, and long bone fractures. Again, balance is the key. Vitamin E, an immune-supporting antioxidant, is

A balance of the proper minerals and vitimins are essential for your Peke's health and development.

and wheat are around 50, and corn is 45.

Carbohydrates are broken into simple sugars, the major source of energy for the body and a source of dietary fiber. Starchy carbohydrates add structure, texture, and form to kibbled food, making the product stable and easy to feed. Carbohydrate excess can occasionally cause obesity. This occurs when your Peke eats more than his energy needs require, and the extra glucose is stored as fat. Most commercial dry dog foods contain between 30 and 70 percent carbohydrates.

Some dog foods are made primarily of grain and other plant products, which makes them less expensive. Inexpensive foods may also have lower-quality protein than some of the more premium brands.

receiving renewed interest for its possible role in preventing several diseases.

Safety

The Food and Drug Administration (FDA) requires that all animal foods, like human foods, be safe to eat, produced under sanitary conditions, contain no harmful substances, and be truthfully labeled. Canned pet foods must be processed to conform to the low-acid canned food regulations to ensure the food is free of viable microorganisms. There is no requirement that pet food products have pre-market approval by the FDA, but the agency does require proper identification of the product, net quantity statement, name and place of business of the manufacturer or distributor, and proper listing of all the ingredients in the product in order from most to least, based on weight. Many of these regulations are based on a model provided by AAFCO.

Commercial Food and the Pekingese

For a healthy Pekingese, a diet consisting of dry food (kibble) is usually the best

Pekingese need a well-balanced diet that provides sufficient calories for growth, activity, and cell repair.

choice. Dry food not only helps reduce buildup of dental tartar and calculus but also promotes firmer, healthier stools. However, if your Peke has dental issues or tooth loss, he may find it easier to chew a softer, canned diet. Semi-moist food, usually sold in small packets, generally contains a lot of sugar and preservatives, so it's probably best to avoid it. Foods with red dye or beet pulp can stain the coat around the mouth and should also be avoided.

The Pekingese mouth, like that of other toy breeds, is small and the teeth are often crowded, scrambled, and subject to dental problems. A smaller kibble will be easier for him to eat. Pekes are often picky, dainty eaters, so you will want the food to be highly palatable, with high digestibility so your Peke will be well nourished.

You can't go entirely by the package label as to how much to feed your dog. The labels are just guidelines and generally suggest a higher portion than your dog should ever eat. The amount and type of food your Peke needs depends on his size, age, build, metabolism, activity level, and any special health issues. Dogs are individuals, just like people. An active dog will need more food than a couch potato, and the Peke can fall into either category.

Noncommercial Diets

Many dog owners choose to cook for their dogs or feed them a raw diet. There are many things to consider before you make this choice.

You saw in the previous section how complex the nutritional requirements are for a good-quality food. The primary concern in the home-made diet is the possibility of errors in calculating energy, amino acids, minerals, vitamins, and fatty acids. Calories in home-prepared diets are not easy to calculate. A miscalculation can lead to obesity when the diet is not balanced by an increase in activity. Obese dogs are prone to osteoarthritis, respiratory distress, cardiac and circulatory problems, diabetes mellitus, liver problems, and immune deficiencies. In the Pekingese, obesity contributes to several breed-specific problems.

If you feed low-quality or incomplete proteins, it could result in amino acid imbalances, causing a decrease in protein synthesis (the way proteins are assembled from amino acids). This in turn can cause poor skin and hair quality, decreased muscle mass, and decreased immune responses. Feeding excess amounts of protein is not likely to be harmful in healthy dogs because the excess is used for energy or is excreted. However, in dogs with renal disease, excess protein may contribute to progression of the disease.

DOG FOOD LABELS

As a general rule, the fewer ingredients listed in the food, the healthier it is. Foods with long lists of ingredients contain more chemicals and by-products. Ingredients must be listed by weight in descending order, so look for a food with more meat protein than grain protein. One or more types of meat, or fish meal or high-quality dairy products such as eggs, should be listed among the first three to five ingredients.

Foods labeled as "complete and balanced" must meet standards established by the Association of American Feed Control Officials (AAFCO), either by meeting a nutrient profile or by passing a feeding trial. There are now two separate nutrient profiles for dogs—one for growth (puppies) and one for adult maintenance. Maximum levels of intake of some nutrients have been established for the first time, including recommendations on protein, fat, vitamins, and mineral content of foods.

The Raw or BARF Diet

Proponents of the raw meat diet claim it improves a dog's performance, coat, body odor, teeth, and breath. While high-performance dogs such as racing Greyhounds and sled dogs have been fed raw meat diets for years, the trend to feed raw meat to companion dogs is a recent phenomenon. This trend has sparked health concerns because of the risk of foodborne illnesses in pets as well as the public health risks of zoonotic infections (those transferred from animal to human).

The presence of *Escherichia coli* (*E. coli*), *Salmonella*, and *Campylobacter* organisms in raw meat is the biggest concern. Parasites and protozoal organisms can be transmitted, even in meat labeled fit for human consumption. Studies have shown that animals fed raw protein diets shed significantly higher amounts of pathogenic bacteria in their stools than those fed cooked proteins. Indications are that this may put some people at risk.

The most popular raw diet is BARF (Biologically Appropriate Raw Food), formulated by Dr. Ian Billinghurst and Robert Mueller, who together have more than 50 years of combined study in raw foods. This diet claims to maximize health and longevity and reduce allergies and vet bills. It is based on the raw foods eaten by dogs' wild ancestors. The food must contain muscle meat, bone, fat, organ meats, vegetables, and fruits. The mixture is based on human-grade whole foods and can be prepared at home or is commercially available.

The Vegetarian Diet

Many people have adopted a vegetarian lifestyle for either health or ethical reasons, and some have chosen to feed their pets this way as well. This is not a decision to be made lightly. For example, a dog's protein and calcium needs are much higher than those of humans. Dogs need vitamin B12, not found in most plants. Essential fatty acids are, well, essential! These nutrients are most easily provided through animal-derived ingredients.

A vegetarian diet, where eggs and dairy products are permitted, is a little easier to follow than a vegan diet, where no animal products are allowed at all.

What are the benefits of a vegetarian diet? Complex carbohydrates are present in the diet to give your Peke energy. Dietary fiber maintains intestinal health. Vitamin A keeps eyes and skin healthy. Vitamin D keeps bones and teeth strong. Vitamin E keeps reproductive and intestinal systems healthy. Vitamin K is good for blood. And B vitamins support almost all areas of health. Foods that provide these benefits are:

Many dog owners choose to cook for their dogs or feed them a raw diet.

- vegetables, especially carrots and green plants
- fruits, though citrus may be toxic to dogs
- some nuts (but not walnuts or macadamia nuts, which are toxic to dogs)
- grains, including brown rice and corn

If grains and vegetables are added to the diet, they generally should be cooked for better digestibility, as they are in commercial foods.

Before you start your Peke on this type of diet, consider this. The ethical consideration of feeding animal products to your Peke should be weighed against feeding a diet that is opposed to what would be consumed in nature. Also, it is best to inform your vet that your dog is on a meat-free diet.

Either way, vegetarian dog treats as supplements are an excellent way to provide snacks that are low calorie and nutritious for your dog.

Should You Free Feed Your Pekingese?

Some owners feed their dogs on a schedule, while others "free feed," which means providing a constant food supply throughout the day. If your Peke is a nibbler and does not overeat, you can put out his day's ration and let him eat whenever he wants. But don't fill the bowl whenever it becomes empty or he will overeat. If you are using canned food, you should not let it remain at room temperature for too long at a time. Free feeding may make it difficult to housetrain your dog; some dogs do better if they can "go" right after they eat.

Table Scraps

Most experts discourage table scraps. If you can't resist, make sure they are low in fat, salt, and sugar, like lean meat or vegetables, and don't make up more than 10 percent of the total diet. Avoid fatty foods like chicken skin or the fat from meat, as they can cause pancreatitis and other gastrointestinal illnesses.

Take into consideration that once you start handing out table scraps, it will be hard to stop. In spite of your Peke's royal heritage, your guests may not appreciate his constant begging. Or worse, they may consider him a common beggar!

Obesity

The complications of obesity in dogs are similar to those in humans—increased incidence of arthritis, diabetes, cardiovascular problems, urinary incontinence, and anesthesia risk. The

Puppy Love

PUPPY FEEDING TIPS

Adhering to a strict feeding schedule for your puppy will aid in housetraining. He will learn to relieve himself right after mealtime and learn good habits early. This is also a good time to teach him not to beg from the dinner table. As hard as it may be, ignore him until he understands that your food is not his food.

Pekingese has additional problems if overweight, including added strain to the spine (causing back problems) and additional pressure on the airways (causing breathing problems).

To tell whether your Peke is overweight, use the Body Condition Scoring (BCS) system. It is easy to do. First, check the ribs by putting your hands on the dog's sides, over the ribs. Rub over the ribs gently. There are 13 on each side. If you cannot feel or count at least three or four ribs, your dog is probably overweight. Next, look at the dog from the side. The abdomen should be tucked up in front of the back legs. Now look from the top. You should see a definite waist behind the dog's ribs. This one may be harder to do with that thick Peke coat!

Before you start your Peke on a weight loss regimen, make sure there are no health problems like low thyroid or other endocrine disorders. Have your vet help you calculate the number of calories your dog should eat per day and recommend a low-calorie food. These diets are usually low in fat and high in protein and nutrients. And start it early—before he becomes dangerously obese.

A few more tips to consider:
• Feed your Peke several small meals a day, as this uses more energy than a large meal.

Don't let your Peke become a couch potato! Exercise him daily for optimal health.

Ask the Expert

OBESITY RISKS IN THE PEKE

Q: What are the dangers of excess weight on my Pekingese?

A: "In addition to the problems all obese animals have, such as more orthopedic disease, more cancer, and more urinary tract disease, Pekingese have their own issues. Their short noses and normal-size tongues and soft palates make for obstructive respiratory problems, even in normal weight dogs. If they are obese, the passages are even more restricted. Pekes have more than their share of back disease, and extra weight compounds this. Also, many have problems with their bowed front legs, and extra weight makes this worse as well. As they get heavier, there are more skin problems due to thicker skin folds."

—Dr. Rick Millen, DVM, Stonecrest Animal Medical Center, Huntington, West Virginia

- Take your dog for walks—it will be good for both of you.
- Make sure everyone in the family follows the rules!

Another idea is to ask your vet about the drug Dirlotapide, which aids in the absorption of fats in the intestine. It tricks your dog's mind into thinking he is full after a small meal. You have to make sure he gets enough nutrition during this regimen, and his diet has to be controlled once he is off the drug or the weight will come back.

The Senior Pekingese Diet

Foods marketed for senior dogs do not have to meet a standard nutritional profile beyond the AAFCO minimum for adult dogs. This is unfortunate because older dogs have similar nutritional needs but need fewer fats and more protein and fiber to aid in digestion. Thinking we are doing the right thing, we might replace a perfectly acceptable adult food with a senior food, assuming it contains less fat or sodium, when this may not be the case.

When planning your senior Peke's menu, avoid excessive carbohydrates and high sugar content; bad fat sources such as animal meal or animal by-products; table scraps and treats made for humans; highly processed foods; treats made with preservatives and fillers; and foods with reduced levels of protein.

As dogs age, they may have a reduced ability to absorb nutrients. This can lead to dry, brittle coats, thickened skin, and susceptibility to skin infections. Too much fat can cause acute or chronic pancreatitis, especially in spayed females.

As dogs age, they may have a reduced ability to absorb nutrients.

Extra pounds (kg) on an older Peke may contribute to joint disease, congestive heart failure, and diabetes. Exercise is a vital part of preventing weight gain, but be sure to limit the intensity of his workouts and gear the activity toward your dog's fitness level and health condition.

Food Allergies

A food allergy results when your dog's immune system over-responds to a food source. This source can be meat, grains, or vegetables. Signs of a food allergy may include dry itchy skin, excessive scratching or licking, bald patches, a high frequency of hot spots, ear infections, skin infections, diarrhea, and vomiting. In addition to being uncomfortable for your dog, excessive scratching will wreak havoc on his coat and skin.

If your vet determines that your Peke has a food allergy, she will likely recommend that you try an elimination diet—feeding a specially formulated food that has a different protein source and a different carbohydrate (grain) source from what your dog has had before. Common anti-allergy foods include kangaroo, oatmeal, venison, fish, duck, potato, etc.

While your Peke is on a special diet, it is important that he doesn't get any other foods such as cookies, treats, rawhides, people food, etc., because you don't know exactly what causes the allergy. Once you have him on a food he is not reacting to, you can start to reintroduce other foods. If your dog has a reaction, you'll know exactly which food causes the problem.

Foods That Are Bad for Your Pekingese

Some foods can cause serious health problems for your Pekingese. These include caffeine, onions, raisins, grapes, macadamia nuts, mushrooms, and the artificial sweetener Xylitol, which can cause low blood sugar and liver failure. Alcoholic beverages are also a no-no. Some of these foods may cause only mild digestive upsets, while others can cause severe illness and even death.

Chocolate is bad for your dog—dark chocolate and unsweetened bakers chocolate being the riskiest. Chocolate is made from cocoa, and cocoa beans contain caffeine and a related chemical compound called theobromine, which is the real danger. Dogs metabolize theobromine much more slowly than humans. Even small amounts of chocolate can cause vomiting and diarrhea. Truly toxic amounts can induce hyperactivity, tremors, high blood pressure, a rapid heart rate, seizures, respiratory failure, and cardiac arrest.

Time is critical if you think your dog has ingested any of these foods. Call your veterinarian or the ASPCA Animal Poison Control Center at (888) 426-4435. Be prepared to state your dog's breed, age, weight, and symptoms, and be ready with all the details of what your Peke has eaten.

Be aware of the foods that can cause serious health problems in your Pekingese.

Chapter
5

Grooming Your
Pekingese

You can tell just by looking at the Pekingese that a great deal of maintenance is involved in keeping him looking his best. This is something you should consider when choosing this breed as your companion. Grooming your Peke, however, can be a pleasurable experience for both of you and a wonderful way to bond.

Your Peke's breeder may have started training your puppy to lie on his side from an early age, making it easier for you to brush and trim him throughout his life. Continue this training from his first day home, even if he doesn't have enough hair to brush. Brushing stimulates blood circulation and can be relaxing for your dog. It also stimulates natural oils and gets rid of loose hair, preventing little tumbleweeds from floating around your house!

Grooming Supplies

Today's grooming supplies have gone far beyond the brush and comb. You can find dog mouthwash, electric toothbrushes, ionizing brushes, aromatherapy shampoos and colognes, bathrobes—you name it.

You can tell just by looking at the Pekingese that a great deal of maintenance is involved in keeping him looking his best.

Check It Out

GROOMING YOUR PEKE

✓ Check your Peke's eyes and wrinkle once a day.

✓ Brush the coat at least several times a week.

✓ Bathe your Peke before he really needs it.

✓ Brush your Peke's teeth daily, or at least once a week.

✓ Perform weekly ear inspections.

✓ Check the pads for mats or small rocks.

If you decide to try your hand at grooming your own Peke, here are some items you should have.

- Baby shampoo or foam wash for around the eyes
- Cornstarch
- Detangling spray
- Ear powder and cleaner
- Flea comb or small cat comb for around the eyes
- Metal comb with both wide and narrowly spaced teeth
- Hair clips large enough to grasp a thick lock of coat
- Hair dryer, your own handheld or a professional pet stand-up dryer
- Nail clippers, either the guillotine or pliers style, or cat nail clippers; a nail grinder is also an option, but you have to be careful not to catch errant hairs in the grinder while using it
- Shampoo and conditioner made for a coated breed
- Slicker brush with a soft pad and flexible pins
- Small round-tipped scissors
- Small good-quality cushion-based steel pin brush (look for the type without knobs on the end of the pins)
- Spray bottle that can lightly mist
- Styptic stick or powder in case of a nail bleed
- Tack box or other container for all of the supplies
- Toothbrush and toothpaste made for dogs

Brushing Your Pekingese

The Pekingese coat reaches full bloom when your Peke is 12 to 14 months old. There is a top coat (long guard hairs) for weather resistance and an undercoat (thick, softer hairs) for warmth and skin protection. The undercoat grows thicker during winters; then it sheds during spring and summer. Unspayed females usually shed at the time of their heat cycle.

You should brush your dog several times a week to get out dead hair and prevent matting. You may discover that you can get

Always wet your Peke's coat before you start brushing.

products attract dirt, making the coat brittle and easier to break off. Use the spray bottle to lightly mist the coat to prevent static, and continue to spray as you brush. The spray bottle can contain tap water, water mixed with a bit of conditioner, or an anti-static conditioner.

Once the coat is wet, brush the underlayer first and then continue to brush layer by layer until each section is finished. Brush from the skin to beyond the end of the hair to prevent breakage. As you get to the harder outer coat, you can switch to the pin brush.

If you find a mat—and you will—sprinkle it with a little cornstarch or spray it lightly with your spray bottle. Try to separate the mat with your fingers or use the end tooth of the comb. Sometimes you may have to cut into the mat. If so, slice it perpendicular to the dog, not across the mat. Separating a mat is an art, and you will soon be a pro if you are patient and figure out which grooming tool works best for you. As tempting as it is to just cut out the mat, keep in mind where it is and how it will look once your dog is all groomed and bathed.

Continue layering and brushing until you have finished the entire dog. Some

by with once a week—it depends on the length, texture, and thickness of the coat.

Resist the urge to grab a brush and start brushing the top layers of your Peke's coat. You will create a disaster if there are mats lurking underneath. You'll need to do a little work before you begin. By now your Peke should be trained to lie on his side or on his back, or stand quietly on a nonskid surface. Using hair clips, section off several top layers of coat so that you have access to the bottom layers. The best tool for grooming the undercoat is the slicker brush. The fine wire pins reach through to the skin to remove loose hair. A slicker with a soft pad and flexible pins will protect the skin.

Next wet the coat. Never brush a dry coat—pollutants, humidity, and styling people start with the tummy, with the dog on his back, and some start with the chest or the back. Find a way that works best for you and your dog.

Thick-coated breeds tend to mat under the legs and around the ears. When you get to these areas, you will need to switch to a smaller brush or comb. These are the most difficult places to work. The ears are very sensitive, so you have to be careful not to injure the tissue with the teeth of the comb. And protect those eyes! Be careful when using any grooming tool around the face.

What About a Short Clip?
Having your Peke clipped short will not save you from brushing. The shorter clips also mat, but they are easier and less time-consuming to keep brushed out and bathed. For the pet Pekingese, these short puppy clips can be great time-savers.

Grooming Table
To make your brushing sessions easier, you may want to invest in a professional fold-up grooming table with a nonslip surface. Another option is a ringside table, a smaller version of the grooming table. They weigh about 10 pounds (4.5 kg) and are completely portable. You can purchase these tables online or from a dog show vendor. You can set up your table in your den and brush your dog at your leisure while watching television. A

lot of breeders and exhibitors do the very same thing! (Note: Never leave your dog unattended on a grooming table.)

Brushing your Peke in your lap is not a good idea. He needs to learn that grooming is an important part of his existence and a separate function from playtime or cuddle sessions.

Bathing Your Pekingese
Since you probably will not be carrying your Pekingese in your sleeve, he will tend to get a little dirty. The key to bathing your dog is to bathe him just before he needs it. But how do you know before your dog

Use a small good-quality cushion-based steel pin brush.

Make sure you rinse the coat thoroughly.

water running over it. If he should tilt his head back, the water could actually run into the dog's lungs and he could drown. I'm not trying to scare you—I'm just letting you know how to protect your dog. A good alternative is to use a cup to rinse your dog so that you can better control the water flow.

Use tearless baby shampoo or foam around the eyes to prevent irritation. Before applying product to the face, place your fingers over the nostrils to prevent anything from running down his nose.

Rinse the coat thoroughly and apply diluted conditioner. Let the conditioner saturate the coat for a few minutes for optimum benefit. Rinse well. Bundle up your dog in a thick towel. But don't towel dry him—that will only cause tangles. Remember the angora sweater!

needs a bath? You will, eventually. It will become instinctive. When the coat starts getting dirty you will see that it is more likely to clump—but this is too late! You need to act when your dog barely starts to feel dirty.

At bath time, place a nonskid mat in the bottom of the sink or tub. Start out by getting just his body, legs, and tail wet. Dilute the shampoo in a separate bottle or cup, as it is hard to get straight shampoo out of that thick coat. Treat the coat as if it were an angora sweater. The gentler you are with the coat, the fewer tangles you will have.

Important Note: Because of the unique head structure of the Pekingese, you should never wash the dog's head with

Drying

Lay the dog on his side. Using your hair clips, pin up the outer layers of coat and dry the undercoat first, brushing it the entire time to keep it straight. Move the dryer slowly over the coat and make sure your Peke's skin does not get too hot. Dry the hair layer by layer until it is all dry.

Even when you think it is dry enough—dry it more. This is one of the keys to preventing mats.

The same principles apply to drying the short coat. You still need to check for mats as you brush, and the coat must be completely dry to prevent future matting.

The best dryer is the type that comes on a stand, leaving your hands free. Some stand dryers are for the floor, others are for the table. Pet dryers are best, as the heat temperature is milder than that from a human hair dryer. You can buy adjustable dryer holders that hold a portable hair dryer in place on your table. Regardless of which type you use, keep tabs on how warm your dog's skin is—you don't want dryer burn

Pekingese to make sure it stays dry and irritation-free.

Trimming Your Pekingese

Because the Pekingese is supposed to have a natural appearance, the American Kennel Club (AKC) standard penalizes any obvious trimming or sculpturing of the coat. Regardless, you will want to trim the coat on the ends of the feet. Unless you trim these "slippers," your poor dog will be tripping over himself. Tidy up the feet by trimming the excess coat into a natural-looking V shape. This will not only be safer for your Peke but will also make it easier to keep his feet clean.

Most Pekingese coats are very forgiving and will survive a few mistakes on your

Washing the Wrinkle

This is a good time to check the wrinkle for any irritation or yeast infections. Wash the area with a mild diluted soap on a soft washcloth, rinse, and make sure the area is dry after the bath. If you see any rawness or irritation, or if there is a yeasty smell, apply oxytetracycline ointment several times a day until it is cleared up. If the ointment does not work, consult your vet. The wrinkle should be checked every day on the

For routine ear cleaning, there are a number of over-the-counter products to use.

Grooming Your Pekingese 61

WRINKLE CLEANING

Q: What is the best way to keep the wrinkle clean on my Peke's face?

A: "The wrinkle extends from one cheek over the bridge of the nose to the opposite cheek. It should be cleansed every day with a mild, diluted soap and wash cloth, or baby wipes, then gently dried. Occasionally, due to moisture, an infection can form in the wrinkle. The dog may rub his face and the area may have an odor; often you don't see anything. You can treat this with a generic oxytetracycline ointment, available over the counter. Apply two or three times a day until the area is healthy. Please consult your vet if the infection is bad or the ointment does not work."

—Carrie Forsyth, Roll-About Pekingese

part. Just relax and enjoy the benefits of your hard work. It will get easier.

Ear Care

Dogs with drop-down ears like the Pekingese are especially susceptible to infections. Make cleaning your Peke's ears less traumatic by handling them gently while you pet him. Check them weekly— they should be clean and pink. If you see a brown or black discharge, it could be ear mites, which can cause intense irritation of the ear canal. Mites will cause your Peke to shake his head and scratch his ears. Redness, swelling, and odor could be a yeast or bacterial infection. All of these conditions require medical treatment.

For routine cleaning, there are a number of over-the-counter products to use, or you can buy something from your vet. Apply the cleanser into your dog's ear canal and massage the base of the ear for 30 seconds to soften and release the debris. Wipe out the loose debris and excess fluid with a cotton puff. Never use cotton tip applicators in the ear canal. They can cause damage. A cotton puff is much safer.

Eye Care

The protruding eyes of the Pekingese require special attention to prevent injuries. Check your Peke's eyes daily for any sign of inflammation, dryness, or eyelashes irritating the eye. If they are bloodshot, cloudy, or partially closed, consult your vet. An emergency situation, which we will talk about in Chapter 9, is any sign of the eye actually coming out of the socket, trapping the eyelids behind it. Yes, it can happen, but there are preventive steps that will be covered later.

To keep your dog's eyes healthy:

- Use your flea comb or cat comb to carefully remove any debris from the corner of the eye and from the eyelashes.
- If there are any errant short hairs at the top of the wrinkle, pluck them if they irritate the eyes.
- Always be careful using any instruments that could cause damage around the eyes.

Eye Stains

Often a light-colored Pekingese will get eye stains, especially when teething. This pinkish pigment is due to oxidation of elements in the tears, much like rusting metal. Keep the area around the eyes as dry as possible with a soft cloth. Some commercial products on the market may help. Puppies usually outgrow eye stains as they get older.

If your Peke still has stains after he has all of his adult teeth, ask your vet about using tetracycline powder orally as an antioxidant. You will be using it at a very low dosage, so you don't have to worry about him building up a resistance. Note: Do not use tetracycline in a dog whose adult teeth have not yet grown in—it can cause discoloration! Hard water can contribute to staining around the eyes and mouth, as well as food or treats with red dye or beet pulp.

Dental Care

The Peke's mouth is small, which means his teeth are close together and often crowded. This can lead to plaque and tartar buildup, and eventually, tooth loss. Dental disease doesn't affect just the mouth. Gum infections can lead to systemic disease by spilling bacteria into the bloodstream, leading to the heart, liver, kidney, and brain, causing damage to those organs.

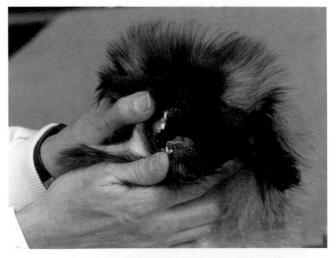

The Peke's mouth is small, which means his teeth are close together and often crowded.

TEETHING PUPPIES

Puppies start to lose their baby teeth at three months of age. Occasionally these teeth are retained when the permanent teeth come in, causing overcrowding and possibly pain and inflammation. Try to wiggle the puppy tooth gently out, but don't force it. Sometimes it is necessary to have the baby tooth removed by your vet.

If periodontal disease develops, the gums will eventually recede, causing tooth and bone loss, bleeding, and pain. Canine dentistry has evolved at about the same pace as human dentistry, so you can take your dog for periodontal surgery, orthodontics, root canals, caps, etc. However, it can be painful for your dog and is very expensive.

Brushing Your Peke's Teeth

Make brushing your dog's teeth part of his grooming routine. Since plaque hardens quickly, brushing daily is best, but if this is not possible, try at least once a week. Use a toothpaste designed for dogs, formulated not to foam. Brush the inner surfaces as well as the outer, and get the crevice where the tooth and gum meet. If a toothbrush does not work well for you,

try dental pads, gauze, or sponges. They are not quite as effective but will help keep the teeth and gums clean. Another option is using enzyme or antibacterial drinking water additives or mouth sprays that help with tartar control. If your dog already has tartar, you won't be able to remove it yourself. A note of caution: If there is a chance your dog will bite you if you try to clean his teeth, don't risk it. Leave this chore to your vet!

Tooth scalers, like the type your dentist uses, are not recommended for your dog. You can easily tear the gum, allowing for infection or bacteria to enter the bloodstream.

Another way to assist in dental care is to give your Peke dry kibble and hard biscuits designed for tartar control. Nylabones and toys with knobby protrusions are designed to keep teeth healthy as well. Beef hooves can also help clean teeth and massage gums as your pet chews. Raw vegetables are also a good choice, and dogs love them.

Rawhide is another product that helps with dental plaque, but please use with caution. The FDA has reported that some rawhide imported from other countries contains bacterial contaminants such as *Salmonella* and even arsenic, lead, and mercury. In addition, rawhide may get caught or even swell inside the digestive tract.

Professional Cleaning

Your vet can tell you whether your dental regimen has been successful. Sometimes genetics will play a role, causing dental issues with even the most meticulous regimen. In this case, a professional teeth cleaning is necessary. The vet will scale and polish the teeth and check for any disease processes. Often a tooth removal is necessary if it is too damaged. Antibiotics are often given before, during, and/or after a dental procedure to prevent bacteria from infecting the gums or leaking into the bloodstream.

Dental procedures are almost always performed under anesthesia. Your veterinarian will examine your Peke to make sure he is healthy enough to undergo anesthesia. A pre-anesthesia blood test is a must. The vet may order other tests, depending on the health of the dog. Though there is some risk associated with any medical procedure, modern anesthesia is usually safe, even for older pets. Because of the unique head shape and occasional breathing problems of the Pekingese, ask your vet about using a gas anesthetic such as Isoflurane that is quickly eliminated from the dog's body once inhalation stops.

Nail Care

Your Peke's nails need to be trimmed on a regular basis. If they become too long they can actually interfere with his walking. Untrimmed nails can even split, resulting in pain and bleeding, or curl under and grow into the pad.

Each nail has a blood vessel called the quick running through the center. The quick contains sensitive nerve endings

Your Peke's nails need to be trimmed on a regular basis.

GROOMING AS A HEALTH CHECK

A good time to do a health check is while you are grooming your Pekingese.

✓ Check the skin for irritation, fleas, ticks, lumps, or anything else out of the ordinary. Dry, dull skin and brittle hair can be a sign of systemic disease or simply a need for a supplement or change in food.

✓ Check the eyes for discharge. Pekes produce tears that can cause clumping at the corner of the eye, and this needs to be wiped away. If the discharge seems excessive, it may be caused by a medical issue like dry eye, allergies, or infection.

✓ Check the teeth for signs of tartar buildup or gum disease. If he has "doggy" breath, he may need to have his teeth cleaned. Or it may indicate a more serious problem affecting body systems such as the liver or kidneys.

✓ Check the ears for signs of redness or swelling. Ear mites and infections require medical treatment.

that, when accidentally clipped, cause pain and bleeding. The prospect of snipping a dog's toenails and causing bleeding is daunting to many pet owners. Even the most seasoned groomer can clip a nail too short. If this happens, use a styptic pen or powder to stop the bleeding. In spite of the blood, it is not as bad as you think. The pain lasts only a few seconds. Sometimes it is worse for the owner than the dog!

Clip the nails with your Peke on his side or standing—whatever works. Hold the paw in one hand and the trimmer in the other. Take a deep breath. The key is to clip the nail to within approximately 2 millimeters of the quick. A Pekingese can have light- or dark-colored nails, even on the same dog. Light-colored nails are easier to cut because you can see the blood vessels and nerves. Cut dark-colored nails in several small cuts to reduce the chance of cutting into the quick.

As you cut the nail deeper, you will see a gray to pink oval starting to appear at the top of the cut surface of the nail. Stop at this point, as additional cutting will cut into the quick. You can file the end of the nail to smooth the cut surface.

Some Pekingese have dewclaws with nails on the front legs or (rarely) on the back legs. Breeders should always have the dewclaws removed shortly after birth to prevent them from scratching the eyes should the dog paw at his face. Dewclaws can also catch on things or rip off in play.

If your dog has dewclaws, those nails have to be clipped as well.

While you are training your dog to lie on his side, get him accustomed to having his feet handled, making it a pleasant experience. Many dogs absolutely hate this part of grooming from the second they see you pick up those clippers. Make him feel secure and praise him every time he lets you finish a foot. Bear in mind that even the best-mannered dog is capable of biting when in distress.

Pad Care

Keep the hair between the pads cleaned out to prevent mats that cause pain when walking. Small round-ended scissors are the safest choice. Hold the scissors parallel to the foot and trim the excess hair. Then, while holding the dog very still, separate the pads and carefully trim out that hair. Be careful! You don't want to nick the delicate skin. Sometimes small rocks or other debris can lodge in the pad area.

Be on the lookout for interdigital cysts, which form between the pads. They can be quite painful and have to be treated with antibiotics and/or removed surgically. Cysts are infections in the sebaceous (oil) glands or the follicles.

And finally, check the pads for drying or cracking. Cocoa butter or shea butter products can help ease the dryness. The pads of the feet act as a shock absorber for the foot and leg and contain eccrine (sweat) glands, which allow a dog to lose heat, or sweat, through his paws.

Professional Grooming

If you love the breed but feel overwhelmed by the coat, a professional groomer is the best option. A groomer can trim your Peke in what is called a "puppy clip," with the coat trimmed roughly the same length all over. The groomer will also clean the ears and trim the nails. You will still need some of the grooming items listed earlier to keep your Peke brushed out between appointments.

Note: Make sure the groomer you choose does not use a cage dryer. Pekingese can easily become overheated and could die from heatstroke!

Whether you decide to let your Pekingese model his magnificent coat and lion mane or send him to the salon for a sportier, trimmer look, your Peke will still be a majestic creature that you will grow to love for himself alone.

Chapter
6

Training Your
Pekingese

The Pekingese have such a regal history and demeanor, sometimes it is hard to think of them as "D-O-G-S." But they are, and we must train them with that in mind. After all, you want your Peke to be well mannered with your guests at home and a good canine citizen in public. A well-trained dog is more likely to be included when you are a guest or go on family outings. If he is trained not to beg, he can stay nearby at mealtime. A socially acceptable pet makes you a socially acceptable dog owner! Further, by developing a strong bond through training, he will learn what is expected of him. This reduces frustration for both of you.

The well-trained Peke who is accustomed to meeting new people and going new places will find a visit to the vet or to a groomer less stressful. Basic obedience commands such as *sit* and *stand* will make a medical exam or a toenail clipping a lot easier. That is not to say he will necessarily stand still the first few times—or ever—but it is a goal you can strive for. Plus, a well-trained dog will be less of a risk of biting someone. It's a terrible thought to bring up, but in this litigious society being a responsible pet owner is an absolute necessity.

If you bought your Peke from a reliable breeder, you probably have a pretty good start. Chances are the breeder spent a lot of time playing with the puppies, teaching basic housetraining, and exposing them to new sights, smells, and sounds and can advise you about the puppy's personality type and any behavior issues you may need to work on. If you did not buy from a breeder, it's not too late to begin his education, even with an older dog. The key is to begin right away and give him the time and attention he deserves.

Whether a puppy or an adult, he needs to learn the rules of the household from the start. What are his toilet options? Which toys are his and which ones belong to his humans? What pieces of furniture can he snooze on, if any? Everyone in the household needs to learn the rules, too, and help the new family member adapt by applying those rules with consistency. Just be firm and don't let him outsmart you with that endearingly ornery face. A well-behaved Pekingese is so much easier to live with than one who is spoiled!

Positive Training

For many years, trainers used harsh methods and negative reinforcement to train dogs, with the understanding that the dog does what you want him to do in order to escape an unpleasant experience, even punishment. Even at its best, dog training consisted of repetitive on-leash obedience drills. Fortunately, in the past few decades positive reinforcement methods have been adapted by many trainers and pet owners and are now the norm.

FINDING A TRAINER

Finding a trainer who understands the behavioral and physical idiosyncrasies of the Pekingese and who trains using positive reinforcement is paramount to your success. The trainer must keep in mind that Pekes cannot tolerate heat as other breeds do, and they lack the stamina of other dogs, so she may have to make adjustments in traditional training methods.

For good training resources, look for books, DVDs, and websites by well-known trainers such as Pat Miller, Dr. Ian Dunbar, Dr. Nicholas H. Dodman, and Victoria Stillwell of Animal Planet.

With positive reinforcement, instead of punishing a dog for doing things you don't want, you reward him for doing things you do want. The reward can be anything the dog really likes, but most trainers use food.

Veterinarian and animal behaviorist Dr. Ian Dunbar revolutionized dog training with his positive motivational approach. In helping create the Association of Pet Dog Trainers (APDT) in 1994, and with numerous public and television appearances, Dunbar is one of the most successful promoters of positive training.

In 1984, Karen Pryor, behavioral scientist and animal trainer, published *Don't Shoot the Dog*, an explanation of "operant conditioning" (isolating wanted behaviors and ignoring the unwanted ones). Pryor is best known as one of the founders of clicker training, which uses a small plastic device that makes a short but distinct "click" sound. This click tells the dog exactly when he has performed a behavior that will earn him a reward. Combined with positive reinforcement, this is an effective, safe, and humane way to teach any animal any behavior it is physically and mentally capable of doing.

Because no force, pressure, pain, or intimidation is used in positive training, the dog learns the behaviors with good associations attached to them.

Socialization

There is a critical period during which puppies need to be socialized by their breeders and their owners. Opinions differ as to exactly when that window is, and it may even vary by breed or by litter. Generally speaking, this period is between 3 and 20 weeks. Learning to coexist, of course, is a lifelong responsibility.

By socialization we mean preparing the puppy for living in a new household and even in society. You want a well-adjusted dog who can interact with the world around him. That doesn't come naturally for all puppies—which is where we humans come in.

Your Peke's breeder should have gently handled your puppy every day, and at age four weeks or so let family members and close friends handle him. He should have been exposed to as many sounds, smells, and sights as possible. The dam of the litter has a role in this process, too. She will typically discipline unsociable behavior like nipping or biting by giving a gentle nip back. Some dams even help paper train their own puppies. That is why it is important to keep the puppies with the mother and with the breeder as long as possible—preferably 12 weeks, but 8 weeks at minimum.

You most likely brought your puppy or adult home in a car, so he has had his first traveling adventure. There will be many car rides in his future, so he needs to get accustomed to those feelings and sounds. If he was afraid, have someone distract him or play with him (in his crate or airline bag) while you are driving.

Once he comes to live with you, he needs to learn the sounds of his new domain—vacuum cleaners, dishwashers, music, doorbells, cars racing by, and children playing in the neighborhood. As much as you try to make all interactions positive, things will likely come up that will upset him. If he cringes from the noises, divert his attention to something more pleasant. If you soothe him or baby him, he may become too dependent on you when upset. If he reacts by barking,

Most trainers now use positive reinforcement methods to train dogs.

he needs to learn when it is appropriate to bark and when it is not. You will eventually discover the best way to console him.

Once your Peke has all of his vaccinations, he will have fun visiting the local dog park or going for a walk around the block to size up his kingdom. You may even find local classes or playgroups for puppies, so you can allow your dog to play and learn with dogs his own age.

A note about vaccinations: Just because your dog is vaccinated doesn't mean he can't pick up a serious illness. Vaccine breaks sometimes occur where the vaccine simply does not work. This is rare but possible. Plus, there are viruses not covered by basic vaccines, and worms and fleas may be present in the soil. Just use caution when you are out with your Peke.

Making Friends With Other Dogs

Your Peke will be meeting a lot of other dogs during his lifetime—at the vet's office, the dog park, or even during a walk around the block. One thing he must learn is "saying hello" on leash. Decide whether sniffing muzzles is allowed. You may want to keep hellos short to prevent either dog from jumping on the other. As small as your Peke is, he would come out on the "short" end of that one. Praise him for a nice hello as you keep moving. If either dog chooses to be rambunctious, remove him from the situation immediately.

A good breeder will have started the socialization process long before you get your puppy

If your Peke will be joining another dog in the household, consider having them meet on neutral territory and give them time to become friends. Then let the new guy enter the house first, leash on, and size up the space. Then bring in the other dog, also leash on, and let them greet each other. The leashes make it possible to separate them if a spat starts—just be careful not to pull hard on the leashes and cause injury. As extra insurance, keep the dogs separated when you leave the house for a few days. Some people do this routinely if there is any doubt they will get along.

Making Friends With Cats

As for cats, let the dog and cat check each other out at a distance, with the dog on a leash in case he bolts after the cat. Maybe even keep the cat in his carrier during these visits. Talk to and pet your dog, getting him relaxed. Give both animals a treat. Repeat these short visits several times a day. Once they get along during leashed visits, try with the dog unleashed (and the cat free) until they accept each other. Don't leave them alone until you are certain they are friends, and make sure they each have their own space.

Oddly enough, a Lhasa Apso I placed in a home with a cat was so smitten with the cat that he actually took him treats and placed them in front of him. This was a real surprise considering how haughty the Lhasa is!

Introducing Children to Your Peke

Since children are above eye level of a Peke and move faster and can be louder, explain to the child that she must approach the dog with kindness and caring. Tell the child to pet the dog only after the dog has seen and smelled the petting hand, then pet him gently. This is a good time to teach the child never to approach a strange dog without permission from the owner. And teach also not to tease or otherwise disrespect the new Peke or any other dog, as dogs are living, breathing beings just as the child is.

Teaching a child or children the safe way to treat your Peke with respect is the best way to ensure their peaceful relationship as long as they are together. And teaching your Peke that children are not to be feared will lessen the chance he will ever threaten a child or end up in a shelter.

Puppies are prone to play-related scratching and biting, so this must be gently discouraged, especially around children and seniors. By the same token, the child must learn how to properly handle the puppy (or adult Peke), and they should not be left unattended until you are sure they both know how to behave! Provide your dog with a quiet retreat area where he can safely go to escape from the commotion if he gets tired or needs a break. Let everyone in the household know that dogs, like humans, need quiet time.

You can teach your child puppy safety by having her help you keep dangerous objects such as small children's toys and food out of the reach of the dog. Another consideration with small children is to make sure they know how to prevent the dog from accidentally escaping through the door. Your curious Pekingese may walk out the front door with no regard for what dangers may lurk outside.

A child who understands the dog's needs can share in the responsibilities of feeding, providing water, walking, and maybe even

PUPPY TRAINING

The younger your puppy is, the more enjoyable his training experience should be. Dogs have very extensive memories, so the fewer corrections you have to make, the better. If your Peke is not doing something you have asked him to do, move on to another exercise or take a break. If you drill and drill a behavior into him, you may lose his attention.

grooming the dog. Taking care of and loving a dog can be the most wonderful experience of a child's life.

Crates—Let the Housetraining Begin!

Crates get a bad rap—they are not "dog jails" unless you make them so. A crate is a very effective way to housetrain your Peke, and if used correctly it will become your Peke's private den. If he travels in the car or stays with you in a motel on vacation, the crate will become a familiar backdrop for an unfamiliar circumstance.

Crate training works for housetraining because the puppy learns that when the urge to urinate or defecate occurs, he can "hold it" to avoid soiling his space (i.e., the crate). He learns that he does not have to relieve himself just because he feels that he needs to.

Choose a crate that allows your dog to lie down comfortably, stand up, and easily turn around. If the crate is too large, he might soil one end of it and sleep at the other. Buy one portable enough that you can carry it into the bedroom at night so that you can hear any signs he needs to relieve himself, like whining, circling, barking, or scratching to go outside.

In order to make the crate a haven, introduce the Peke to the crate simply by leaving the door open and hoping he wanders inside on his own. Praise him for going inside. If he doesn't go on his own, place some treats, his favorite toy, or even his blankie inside and wait for him to go in. Most dogs are enticed by the open door and soon see the crate as an escape from their humans.

Don't keep your Peke in the crate too long. The rule of thumb is that puppies can "hold it" for a time span equal to one hour for each month of age, plus one. Therefore, a three-month-old puppy should be able to control his bladder and bowels for up to four hours.

Housetraining Your Peke

If your puppy has been crated overnight or for a few hours during the day, he will probably be very anxious to get out and go to his designated area. Get him outside right away. At the door, ask "Outside?' Then as you go out, repeat. Watch him to make sure he takes care of business. You may want to train him to go to a certain part of the yard for convenience of cleaning up. Be sure to reward him for going in the right place.

Take him out right after he has eaten, after playing, and after napping. First thing in the morning and last thing at night are also important times. As he grows to adulthood, he won't need all of these trips to the great outdoors.

Don't punish your dog for housetraining mistakes.

It is hard to say how long a healthy dog will take to housetrain. A Pekingese has a smaller bladder than a larger dog, so allow several weeks or even months. However, he might surprise you and take to it very quickly!

When Accidents Happen

Don't punish your puppy if you catch him in the act! Interrupt him by telling him gently "No" and take him outside. When he goes in the proper place, praise him enthusiastically or give him a treat.

If he has an accident but you do not catch him making a mess, don't yell or punish him. Clean it up and forget it. He will have no idea what the scolding is for. He doesn't have the capacity to put the punishment together with something he has done more than a few minutes ago. Using an enzymatic cleaner on the area to clean up the odor will help keep him from going back to the original spot.

Indoor Training

Some owners of small dogs opt to use piddle pads or newspapers throughout the life of the dog. In some cases, such as apartment living, this is necessary, and with travel it can be a real convenience. Piddle pads have a nonskid plastic backing, absorbent layers, and leakproof edges. Some are scented so that dogs will be attracted to them. You can buy a plastic bed to anchor the pad in. There

TRAINING THE PEKINGESE

"**P**ekingese are known to be endearingly stubborn but are actually highly intelligent. They make us work for them, while other breeds work for us by doing what we ask of them without question. Pekingese were highly guarded in palaces and treated like royalty while other dogs were out working. Dogs with this history need to be trained a little differently. They need to have a good reason to get off their fluffy pillows. It's really a lot of fun trying to outsmart the Pekingese. It may take more time, but when you finally do, you will have a great deal of satisfaction and will be a better trainer."

--Pat D'Arcy, Pekingese trainer and exhibitor

are even dog litter boxes and sod systems for indoor pottying. Newspapers are not a good choice for a light colored dog, as the ink will rub off on his coat.

However, if you can avoid indoor training, do so because once the behavior goes on for a long time it may be difficult to change. Also note that indoor training is no substitute for taking your dog for a nice walk.

When It's not the Training

If your puppy seems to have a particularly difficult time with his housetraining, make sure there is no underlying health problem like a urinary tract infection or a kidney problem. Your vet may perform a urinalysis and blood panel to make sure.

Another cause of accidents in the house is submissive urination. This is an entirely different situation from that of a dog who isn't housetrained—it's a behavioral problem. These dogs usually wet themselves or the floor when you first greet them. They either squat or roll over on their back and dribble, a behavior that may date back to the dog's days as a puppy when his mother cleaned him. Scolding him only reinforces the behavior. Consider whether a particular action on your part may be making it worse, or perhaps an object you are carrying is making him fearful.

Try ignoring him when you first get home. Be very low key. Let him come to you and have him sniff the palm of your hand. Stoop down gently and pet him under the chin so that he will feel calm. Then proceed with letting him out to his yard or walking him. Having your visitors do the same will also help the situation.

NO JERKING!

Don't forget—there should be no jerking on the leash while teaching any of these exercises. Not only will it backfire by causing your Peke to lose his trust in you, but a hard jerk on the neck can affect his breathing or even cause trauma to his eyes.

Training Your Pekingese

Historically, Pekingese probably never had to do anything for anyone—so this whole training thing is new to them.

How Long?

For some Pekes, their lack of stamina prohibits long stretches of training. Their rolling gait requires more energy than a typical canine stride. And their nearly flat faces make it difficult for them to get enough air into their lungs for heavy-duty workouts, so they become overheated and breathless very quickly. Pekes with longer noses and larger nares (nasal openings) can work for longer periods of time, as can those with their coats clipped short.

Regardless of your dog's physical structure, the Pekingese personality will always surface. Be prepared to sweet-talk him into understanding why you are asking him to do whatever it is you're asking him to do. Keep your training session upbeat. Once he is convinced of the why, prepare for the how. Pekingese have a more human way of approaching

the challenges of training. They like to think they are training you, so try letting your Peke set the pace. As one trainer says, "Ask them to comply and perhaps they will. Order them and you'll walk the heeling pattern by yourself!"

Obedience components are best taught in small increments over short time spans. With any exercise, if your Peke isn't doing something new you're trying to teach him, back up and work on an exercise you know he can do well. If you just drill and drill you will lose his attention and interest. Remember, we are using positive training methods. Rather than making him do commands, you are helping him succeed so that you can reward him and he'll be eager to do them again. And don't lose your temper! Your Peke needs to know his training environment is safe and stress free. He must be able to trust you.

Rewards

Unless you plan to train your Peke for the obedience ring, use small pieces of cheese, hot dog, or whatever he likes to entice him to learn. (Food is not allowed in the obedience ring.) If you want to wean your dog off food rewards, start rewarding him with lots of praise along with the treat, then treat him intermittently. Or give him the command and occasionally walk over to the cookie jar to get him a treat. He will want to obey "in case" he gets the reward.

Rewarding your dog with praise alone works very well, too. Some dogs are just as happy with that extra-special attention. Pekingese are such hams, the attention they get from being praised will more than likely make them learn quickly. They are not going to think of these actions as commands but as ways to show off.

Location

Vary the location where you practice the exercises. Your dog may stay perfectly in your kitchen but may find too many distractions in other environments. Try the backyard, near playgrounds, and the park, and always use his leash unless it is a fenced-in area.

Tools

While some people use a metal training collar for training many breeds, it is a no-no for a Pekingese because of the possibility of injuring his trachea or affecting his breathing. Use a flat collar or a rolled nylon collar along with a standard leash, preferably 6 foot (2 m).

Basic Obedience Commands

There are six basic obedience commands every dog should learn. Four of them— *down, stay, come,* and *leave it*—could literally save your dog's life, not to mention keep your Peke from being an irritant when you have company. The other two—*sit* and *heel*—come in handy in a lot of situations, including going for a walk.

Sit

The *sit* command is useful for keeping your Peke from jumping up on a visitor or getting him to sit still at the vet's office or at a photo shoot. You can start training your dog to sit when he sits on his own. When you catch him in the act of sitting, say "Sit" and immediately praise him. See how you can make him think it was his idea? Eventually you can ask him to sit for longer periods of time.

If you are unable to capture that moment when your Peke sits, you can teach the command on your own. With a treat in your hand, hold it above his head (but not so high that he'll want to jump for it) and move it back. That should automatically cause him to sit. Say "Sit!" and give him the treat only if he's in the sitting position. If he gets up, try again. Start with a small amount of time to hold the *sit*—15 seconds, 30 seconds, and then work up to 1 minute.

The *sit* command is useful for keeping your Peke from jumping up on a visitor.

If you plan to try your hand at obedience trials, shoot for a one-minute *sit* and you will be ahead of the pack when your dog starts school.

Down

The *down* command can be a lifesaver if your Peke should escape from his yard or get loose from his leash during a walk. If he knows the *down* command and you see him nearing a busy street or other danger, you can immediately yell "Down!" and he will go down and stay until you can get to him and put his collar back on or pick him up. After your heart stops frantically beating, be sure to praise him

for a job well done. (Don't punish him for escaping. It will be the *down* that he will associate with the praise.)

As we discussed with the *sit* command, the easiest way to teach *down* is by taking the opportunity to say "Down!" precisely when he lies down on his own. Then praise and reward him.

If you can't catch him in a *down*, you may have to entice him to go into a *down* position with a treat. Lower the treat to the ground in front of his paws to help get him into the *down*. Repeat as often as you need to but not so much that he gets bored and tired. And never push him down; gently guide him if necessary.

If you have plans to train your dog in obedience, go ahead and work on having him stay down for three minutes, the requirement for the first level, Novice A. Omit the treats or wean him off them. You will be ahead of the game when classes start.

Down can be a confusing command because some dog owners will use it to mean "get off the couch," or "stop jumping on me," as well as "lie down." Make sure everyone in the family uses the term properly so that your Peke will not be confused.

Stay

The *stay* command, much like *sit*, can be used to keep your dog from running toward an open door or bothering visitors.

It can be used with the *sit* or the *down*. For example, stand in front of your dog and tell him to sit. Once he is securely in his sit, stretch out your arm with your palm facing your dog and say "Stay!" Take a few steps back and repeat the command. If he gets up, start over, beginning with the *sit* command. You can increase the distance and time as you go along. This is not an easy exercise, especially if your dog senses you aren't serious enough or are admiring his cuteness. Many otherwise perfect obedience ring performances have been marred by a dog not staying on command. Perhaps they innately want to be with us. Just don't get discouraged with this one. He will obey in time!

Come

The *come* command, also known as the *recall* in obedience training, could be a lifesaver if your Peke gets loose. Plus, if he learns this command well, he will have more opportunities to play off leash in safe areas.

Come can be taught by placing your Peke in a *sit-stay* in a safely enclosed area and walking a few feet (m) away. Say "Come!" and take a few steps back. Use a squeaky toy, treat, or amusing noises, whatever it takes to make him come to you. Praise him enthusiastically. Repeat and gradually increase the distance between you. This exercise can also be taught with the dog on a long leash for

The easiest way to teach *down* is by taking the opportunity to say "Down!" when he lies down on his own.

better control. Gently guide your Peke with the leash if you have to, but do not pop or pull it. You can also squat down and open your arms to him, praising him when he arrives.

Never punish your Peke for coming to you, even if he has escaped the lead or run away! No punishment or intimidation should ever be associated with this command. He must always know that being with you is a happy, safe, and wonderful thing to experience. If your Peke is stubborn and will not come when you ask him to, or you have called him away from a dangerous situation, go to him, put on his leash if necessary, guide him back to where you called him from, and praise him. This teaches the dog that he must follow the command but that you are not angry about it.

Leave It

We have all done it—dropped something on the floor that could be harmful to a dog: medication, a battery, a hot cooking utensil, or a human food not on your dog's diet. Or during a walk in the park your Peke comes across something unsavory that he thinks looks yummy. (After all, dogs don't know what is good for them.) The *leave it* command can be a lifesaver in these situations.

To teach *leave it*, start by putting your Peke on a short leash and dropping a "good" treat on the floor. As he starts for the treat, say "Leave it!" and reward him immediately with a better treat and praise him. Gradually increase the time before he gets the good treat and then train him without his lead. For best results, practice in various locations where he may come across something he shouldn't have.

Heel

Having your Peke walk nicely alongside you instead of

If your Peke knows how to walk nicely on leash, your walks together will be fun.

TRAINING "DO'S"

✓ Teach your Pekingese basic manners so that he will be a good host and a welcome visitor.

✓ Use positive training methods that have replaced the harsher training techniques of the past.

✓ Expose your puppy to different noises, places, and people to improve his confidence when out in the world.

✓ Housetrain your Peke using a crate for best results.

✓ Teach basic obedience commands to keep your dog safe.

✓ Show off your well-trained Pekingese—he will make you proud with his intelligent and regal demeanor.

in front of you will help you navigate in crowds. It will also keep him from straying into the path of others and possibly becoming injured. In dog terms, this is called the *heel*.

The first thing to remember about heeling is that the dog walks on your left side, not your right side. Hold the leash in your right hand while taking up its slack in your left. With your Peke sitting at your left side, say "Heel!" in a bouncy voice. If he walks alongside you, praise him. If he pulls or lags, tell him no and start over. This is usually a pretty easy thing to teach. As you continue with your walks, you can practice keeping him closer to you for his safety.

Make sure you don't pull on his lead hard enough to hurt his neck. Before long he will enjoy his walks so much that you may not have to keep using the command.

Upping the Ante

Eventually increase your Peke's skill level by having him sit or lie down for a longer period of time, or come from a farther distance away. Add distractions like having other people walk around, talk, and maybe even call him away from you. Keep in mind that your job is to train him, not trick him, so make his road to success as easy as possible. The key is consistency and adding new tasks gradually, plus plenty of rewards for good behavior.

Every dog is an individual, so you will need to assess your Peke's personality and determine which training method is best for you on each of these exercises. But if you take the time to train your dog, the payoff will be amazing. You and your Peke will have a greater bond, and he will make you proud with his intelligent and regal demeanor.

Chapter 7

Solving Problems
With Your Pekingese

D ogs are relinquished to shelters and rescue groups for a number of reasons, but one of the most avoidable is lack of training. Once that cute fluffy puppy becomes an adult, the jumping, nipping, and barking aren't so cute anymore. He becomes a nuisance to the family, so they turn the dog over to someone else to deal with. What the owner doesn't realize is that a little training and guidance could have produced a wonderful well-trained canine companion.

The positive reinforcement techniques discussed in Chapter 6 are the best ways to approach unacceptable behavior. Those techniques allow the dog to think about his choices and choose the behavior that pays a reward. Keep in mind that positive reinforcement does not mean the dog is never reprimanded. It means that adding something positive, a treat or praise, will increase the likelihood that a good behavior will recur.

Most behaviors can be corrected with a little patience and understanding. And even old dogs can be taught new tricks in the case of adopting an older Pekingese.

Barking (Excessive)

The dog's ancestor, the wolf, and other wild canids bark very little. Through domestication and by breeding dogs to bark for special purposes, we have created a companion who sometimes barks a lot more than what we want. Normally the Pekingese is not what you would call a "yappy" dog. He usually barks at the proper time, and with reason. However, like other dogs he is capable of unnecessary barking.

Alert barking can be a good thing when you have a not-so-welcome visitor. Dogs have prevented plenty of burglaries. But when your Peke carries on every time someone sets foot on your property, the noise and accompanying behavior become a nuisance. Persistent barking is not good for your dog either, as it could be causing him stress.

What's Causing the Barking?

The first thing to consider is whether there is an obvious cause for your Peke's barking. Does he feel as if he is not getting enough attention? Is he bored? Does he need to go out to relieve himself? Is he in pain or discomfort? Is he annoyed by neighborhood noises that you can't even hear? Is the bark aggressive, warning some perceived threat away? Many of those issues are easily solved by just paying attention to what triggers your Peke's barking.

Sometimes we unknowingly reward barking. When a very young puppy starts barking, we think it is charming and laugh and pay him attention, and he barks more. Then he does it to demand attention, and it is still somewhat cute. He learns eventually that all he has to do to get attention is bark. After all, that is his main form of communication, so how can it be so wrong?

Solutions

First, don't punish your dog for barking. If he is doing it to get attention, even negative attention may be welcome.

The key to dealing with alert barking is to be able to turn it off. If your Peke appears to be barking to alert you, try training him to accept "good dog" or "thank you" for performing his duty

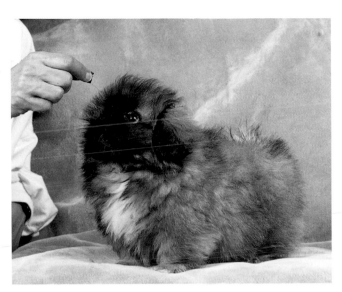

Teach your Peke not to bark by rewarding him when he's quiet.

when he first begins to bark. If this does not work, say "Enough!" or "Use your inside voice!," and give him a reward after he has stopped barking for five seconds or so. It may take quite a few attempts for him to understand what you want.

Some dog owners have success using a shaker can to interrupt barking. Use an empty soda can filled with a few coins or small pebbles. When your dog starts barking, give him a command, such as "No bark," and shake the can. The noise should startle him and distract him from his barking. Once he has stopped barking, praise him and reward him with a treat. When it comes to nuisance barking, remember to reward your Peke for

remaining quiet in a situation where he's normally noisy. If he is barking for no reason you can discern, try calling him to you and have him sit quietly, then reward him with a treat. But you'll have to be careful with this technique. Pekes are smart little creatures—don't let him train you to give him a treat just for barking!

Some barking behaviors may require the assistance of a veterinarian or behaviorist. Dogs will bark if they are deaf because they cannot hear themselves. A trainer or behaviorist can show you how to communicate with hand signals, which should help curb a deaf dog's problem barking. Barking that seems purposeless can be the result of canine dementia.

CONSISTENCY

Consistency is the key to training a happy, well-behaved puppy. Dogs love routine. Schedule your Peke's daily feeding, walking, grooming, and play activities and stick to them as much as possible. Encourage all family members and guests to use the same commands to communicate with your puppy so that he doesn't become confused. For example, you need to figure out whether "down" means get off the couch or lie down. Don't use the same command to mean two different actions.

Repetitive barking for long periods of time that is accompanied by pacing and spinning may be caused by obsessive-compulsive disorder. Most importantly, monitor aggressive barking carefully to make sure the bite doesn't become worse than the bark!

Chewing

Chewing is a completely normal behavior for puppies. However, it can become more of a problem if the pup is bored or has excess energy.

Solutions

With a chewing puppy, your first thought should be prevention. Make sure your home is puppy-proofed and that he does not have access to dangerous or inappropriate items such as electrical cords or trash cans. Keep your clothes and shoes off the floor and safely put away in closets. For when you are not there to monitor him, bitter-tasting spray can be used on items as a deterrent to chewing.

Because chewing is normal, if you find your puppy chewing on something he shouldn't, don't punish him. Instead, say "No!," then offer him something he is allowed to chew, such as a Nylabone. Reward him for playing with or chewing the new item.

Puppies particularly like to chew when they are teething. You can't blame them—just as their 28 baby teeth come in, the 42 adult teeth start coming to the surface. One solution is to dampen a washcloth, twist it, then place it in the freezer for a few hours. Once it is nice and firm, offer it to the puppy to soothe his gums. Ice chips may also work. Massage his gums if he

will let you. Even an older dog may start chewing if his gums hurt or if he has a loose tooth.

Sometimes destructive chewing by puppies or adults can be caused by separation anxiety or even simple boredom. Remember that dogs do not chew to retaliate—they have no concept of spite. Chewing just helps relieve stress. Make sure the dog has plenty of his own "stuff" to play with, and spend time with him playing and exercising. Make his life as full as possible to cut down on the frustrations that lead to excessive chewing.

Coprophagia

Coprophagia, or eating feces, most likely goes back to behavior in the wild where wolves and other canids had to scavenge for survival purposes, as well as hide evidence that they were present. It simply is not an abnormal behavior to the dog. However, this behavior will make you think twice about your Peke's desire to kiss you!

Solutions

Poor diet or underfeeding can contribute to feces eating; other causes may be an unbalanced or poorly digestible diet, pancreatic enzyme deficiencies, or malabsorption (difficulty absorbing nutrients from food). The dog's stool should be checked for parasites and *Salmonella*, which may also be the culprits.

If medical causes for coprophagia are ruled out by your vet, supervision is the answer. Limit your Peke's access to poop. Try training him to sit for a special treat immediately following each bowel movement; it may become a permanent habit. Another option is to try the *leave it* command and then clean up the area quickly.

Some dog owners get results by changing their dog's diet or adding meat tenderizer or papaya to the food to help increase protein digestion, resulting in a less edible stool. Try adding more fiber or switch to a "free feed" regimen so that he always has something to eat.

Digging

Pekingese aren't inclined to tear up the yard, but it can happen. A Pekingese may dig to feel the cool earth, hide a toy, or just because he is bored. If he isn't neutered, he may try to dig under a fence as part of his quest for a mate.

You want to work on this problem right away, as a Pekingese may inhale dirt particles or small pebbles into his nasal passages or even his lungs and create severe health problems. At the very least, all that unnecessary dirt will make grooming your Peke a nightmare.

Solutions

As with many other problem behaviors, supervision is key. Your Peke should not

Playing in the yard with your Peke can be fun, but don't let him start digging—the dirt particles he can inhale can cause health issues.

be left outside unattended anyway, so you should be there to stop any unwanted digging. If you do catch him digging in the yard, take him away from the area, make sure he doesn't have any dirt in his nostrils, and give him other things to do, like playing with his outside toys.

A small edging fence will keep him away from the most tempting places to dig. Spread ground hot chili peppers over the soil for a nasty-tasting mouthful. Make sure you are not making your garden extra attractive to a dog—fertilizers containing bone meal are appealing to dogs, but ingesting them can cause an obstruction in the gastrointestinal tract. And fertilizers may contain iron or disulfoton, which can be poisonous to a dog. There are varieties of mulch,

especially those containing cocoa, that many dogs find appealing but are extremely harmful. And don't forget the dangers of insecticides and pesticides.

Growling and Nipping

There are perfectly understandable reasons for a dog to growl. Puppies play growl, as with tug-of-war. A dog in pain may growl if you try to touch him. A dog with vision or hearing loss may find his surroundings threatening. However, unless you know your Peke's intentions when he growls, you should take his growling seriously. It is not common for a Peke to behave in a vicious manner, so it may be wise to investigate any change in behavior and make sure nothing unusual is going on.

A low-pitched growl or snarl is most likely a warning sign. Dogs signaling with a low pitch from deep in their chest are trying to make themselves appear larger and more dangerous than they really are. This is typically a warning to "back off," and when it happens it is best to give your Peke his space. In fact, it is best to ignore him completely rather than risk a confrontation. Change the subject and wait until he is back to his old self.

Sometimes growling can lead to nipping, and obviously you want to "nip" this in the bud before it leads to biting. Nipping begins in the litter box when the puppies mouth and chew on their littermates, mother, and everything in sight. While nursing, especially when the puppy teeth begin coming in, some puppies bite too hard and the mother reprimands with a nip. Littermates will nip each other as a response to a play bite. This is when bite inhibition develops in most puppies.

Take advantage of this natural training by teaching the puppy that any communication by mouth is unacceptable. No, you don't have to bite back! But do tell the puppy "No!" in a voice slightly louder than your normal voice and ignore him for a few minutes. If this does not work, crate him for a short time. Be consistent and follow through every time. Let visitors who play with the puppy know to do this as well. This is a crucial time to stop mouthing behavior before the puppy becomes a biting adult.

Teeth are an important tool to dogs—a way to communicate. Any dog can bite under the right (or wrong) circumstances, especially if he's in pain or feels threatened. Different dogs have different pain and threat thresholds, but generally speaking, a well-socialized puppy will grow up to be a well-behaved, nonbiting adult.

For more information on behavior modification for nipping problems check out the "Ask the Expert" sidebar from Victoria L. Voith, DVM, Ph.D., one of the pioneers in the fields of applied animal and veterinary medical behavior.

Puppies usually learn bite inhibition from their littermates.

Ask the Expert

Q: How do I keep my Pekingese from nipping my fingers when I try to pet him?

A: "If your Pekingese is a puppy, he may be trying to initiate play. If so, when he is in such a mood keep redirecting him to toys to grab. A loud yelp or 'NO' may also be helpful, but do not use this as your only approach—the puppy also needs readily available toys, exercise, the opportunity to explore novel environments, and acceptable ways to play with you. Contrary to popular belief, tug-of-war does not cause dogs to become aggressive. Be careful not to pull too hard, and personally, I think it is okay to let the dog win. 'Roughhousing' or teasing your puppy with your hands will, however, encourage him to nip at your fingers. Be sure to monitor how people, especially children, play with your dog.

"If your dog nips because he is afraid of being touched, behavior modification using positive reinforcement techniques can usually correct the problem; you may need the help of a professional behaviorist to assist you with this. If the nipping is not related to fear or play and he is exhibiting aggression in other circumstances, a comprehensive behavioral management program may be necessary and you should seek help from a competent professional. A technique that is often incorporated in such programs is 'Nothing in life is free.' First the dog learns the *sit* command. Then whenever he wants something he must sit before he gets it. For example, have him sit before the door is opened to go out or in; before he is allowed up on the sofa; when he asks for attention; periodically during play; before throwing the ball, etc."

—Victoria L. Voith, DVM, Ph.D., Professor,
College of Veterinary Medicine
Western University of Health Sciences, Pomona, California

Housesoiling

A Pekingese puppy should be pretty well housetrained within two to three months after he comes to live with you. Of course, this depends a lot on how old he was, how much training the breeder gave him, and what kind of conditions he grew up in. In general, a puppy should be trained by age four months and have full bladder control by age six months.

Is There a Medical Reason?

If your housetrained Peke starts having accidents in the house, or if your puppy simply cannot become housetrained, there may be an underlying medical cause. Epilepsy can cause involuntary urination or defecation, as can spinal cord injuries and disease. Viral or bacterial infections can cause loose stools or diarrhea. Medical "excuses" even crop up in puppies, such as the congenital deformity known as an ectopic ureter (where the ureter bypasses the bladder). This problem can be corrected by surgery.

If your dog is a senior, incontinence may be a problem. An elderly dog who is showing signs of cognitive dysfunction, or "doggy Alzheimer's," may start to forget his housetraining.

Is It Marking Behavior?

Unneutered males may engage in marking. Canine urine contains many pheromones, chemicals derived from testosterone, which serve as "calling cards" to other dogs. Sometimes marking is accompanied by pawing or scratching to define the territory. Typically, if you neuter a male Pekingese while he is very young, he will never pick up the habit of marking his territory. Sometimes even older dogs will stop the behavior after being neutered. Unfortunately, the problem isn't always solved this easily.

Dominant females may mark, too, so don't be surprised to see your female lift her leg. Females produce small quantities of testosterone in addition to their own scent, which signals they are ready to mate. Spayed females usually cease this behavior, though occasionally they will urine mark when stressed, or have accidents as the result of an age-related drop in estrogen levels.

For male Pekes, belly bands wrap around the mid-section, covering the penis. This will not stop him from hiking his leg, but it will catch the urine if he does. The liner (a mini-pad) of the belly band needs to be changed as necessary. For females, panties or diapers act as a deterrent.

Sometimes it is necessary to go back to "square one" and make sure your Peke knows the appropriate elimination spots and is getting enough opportunities to go out. Confine your Peke to one area of the house, or use baby gates or an ex-pen. Another option is to try using a lead while he is in the house so you will have control at all times.

Reprimand your male (kindly!) when he marks in the house, but praise him when he marks in an appropriate place outside, for example a tree. The message is that urine marking isn't bad as long as it is outside; it's inside the house that's the bad idea.

Be sure to clean up the urine marks with an enzymatic or bacterial product that will destroy the odors at the source. Simply masking the scents will not work.

Your veterinarian may recommend drug therapy for elimination problems. It works by stabilizing the dog's mood, increasing his confidence, or in females, toning the bladder sphincter. Anxiety-reducing drugs may also be effective when used simultaneously with training.

Jumping Up

Dogs love to jump up on people, especially to greet their owners when arriving home. Granted, a small Pekingese bouncing off your legs is not as annoying as an 80-pound (36-kg) dog, but visitors may not like it.

Solutions

When your Peke jumps up on you, do not react. Avert your eyes and adopt an indifferent posture. Don't give him any attention until he stops the behavior, then reward him with a treat when he's not jumping. All family members and visitors need to take part in this training as well—

Dogs love to jump up on people, especially to greet their owners when arriving home.

explain that they need to ignore him until he's behaving appropriately. It's the best way to communicate to your Peke that this behavior is not acceptable.

Another method is to train your Peke to sit before the visitor comes inside, and reward him when he complies. Like most other positive training methods, this rewards an alternative behavior—sitting—and will increase your chance of success. If your Peke persists in jumping up, and if he is trained to heel and sit, correct him by saying "Off!" and then walk him briskly in a circle, tell him to sit, and reward him. Repeat the exercise as long as it takes for him to understand.

Above all, be consistent. Allowing the jumping even just once in five times is enough for the dog to think it may be all right after all.

Obsessive-Compulsive Disorder

The Pekingese is not genetically predisposed to obsessive-compulsive disorder (OCD), but theoretically any dog can show signs of this disturbing ailment. Dogs from puppy mills or shelters, rescue dogs, and those who are confined, bored, or anxious are likely to develop OCD.

Signs are fence-running, pacing, spinning, tail chasing, snapping at imaginary flies, licking, and barking and chewing, especially the paws or flank. The chewing may start after an

WHEN TO SEEK PROFESSIONAL HELP

Some of the behaviors discussed in this chapter are difficult to deal with, and you may find that you need expert help. A good professional trainer or behaviorist has years of experience working with dogs and is familiar with their thought processes. As long as the professional uses positive reinforcement and good communication with you and your dog, getting help can be a worthwhile experience. Just be aware of the methods the professional is using and make sure the problem is not progressing. You want to do everything you can for your Peke!

injury, then never stop. The dog may lose weight, suffer from exhaustion, and even physically injure himself. Often dogs will learn to control their behavior in the presence of the owner but then do it when alone.

Stress and anxiety, as well as physical trauma and illness, can trigger the behavior. Males with OCD outnumber females three to one, and it usually shows between ages one and four. It is very difficult to change. Sadly, many dogs are given up due to OCD.

There has been some success in treating OCD using a combination of drugs and behavior modification. Few completely stop the behavior, but they have shown improvement. Some dogs respond best to distractions, such as being played with or taken out for a nice long walk. Others respond better to an increase in exercise or a calmer, more soothing and predictable home environment.

Separation Anxiety

Why some dogs develop separation anxiety and others do not is unclear. Most puppies survive being separated from their mothers, and after a period of adjustment, from their breeder into a new home. With separation anxiety a dog becomes overly dependent on his owner, and problem behaviors result when he is left alone.

A dog with separation anxiety usually begins exhibiting problem behaviors immediately after the owner leaves. The dog will whine, bark, cry, chew, salivate, scratch the door where you exited, and break housetraining. As tempting as it is, if we go back into the house to try to calm him, we just reinforce the behavior. If we draw out the goodbyes, it makes leaving more obvious.

Solutions
Practice the actions associated with your

leaving without opening the door. Put on your shoes, pick up your keys, and walk to the door, but don't leave. Sit on the couch for a few minutes. Then calmly get up and leave without saying goodbye. Come back inside after a random amount of time, then leave again. You may need to do this several times per day for weeks to quell your dog's anxiety. You can also exit via a door you don't normally use. Wait one minute and then walk back in. If your dog doesn't appear anxious, try two minutes, and keep adding time if the dog continues to be comfortable with it. Practice as many times as needed. Back off on your time, however, if the dog becomes stressed.

When you get home, don't make a fuss about arriving. Condition your dog to think that your arrival and departure are not a big deal.

Other ideas to help a dog with separation anxiety include:

- Get him accustomed to staying alone from the time you bring him home so that your departure won't be new to him.
- Give him some exercise or take him for a walk before you leave. Being tired will help him relax.
- Leave the radio or television on when you leave if he is used to hearing it.
- Use a word as a cue. Say "I'll be back" or "I'm going to work" every time you exit.

If your dog's behavior changes abruptly, it is best to have your vet rule out seizures, diabetes, or other illnesses that could cause the problems you are finding

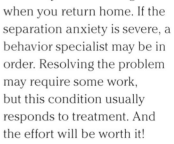

when you return home. If the separation anxiety is severe, a behavior specialist may be in order. Resolving the problem may require some work, but this condition usually responds to treatment. And the effort will be worth it!

Thunderstorm Phobias

One of the most common phobias in dogs is the fear of thunderstorms. Studies have shown that dogs being

If your dog's separation anxiety is severe, a behavior specialist may be in order.

Check It Out

PROBLEM BEHAVIOR CHECKLIST

✓ Train your Peke not to bark by using a key word, like "enough," to let him know when to stop.

✓ Offer your dog a toy in exchange for something he should not have, and praise him for taking the new object.

✓ Don't let your Peke dig in the dirt, as he could inhale particles that could cause harm to his lungs.

✓ Rule out any medical reasons for accidents in the house before proceeding with training.

✓ Nip nipping in the bud before it progresses to biting or other forms of aggression.

✓ Seek the help of a behaviorist if you have problems you cannot control.

✓ Do not give up on your Peke! You will be glad you made the extra effort.

petted during thunderstorms produce more neurotransmitters and hormones associated with good feelings and social bonding. Therefore, if possible, soothe your Peke when you hear that storm brewing.

Behaviorists don't know what it is about this natural phenomenon that causes dogs such grief. Are they reacting to lightning flashes and the sound of thunder, or is it the sudden drop in air pressure? Do they feel the static charge buildup?

Signs of distress in a thunder-phobic dog include head lowering, flattened ears, crouching, shivering, tail tucking, sweaty paws, and even leaking of urine.

Solutions

Of course, if you are fearful during a storm, your Peke will sense your fear. Try slowing down your breathing and your movements, and speak calmly to him.

One approach is to provide a distracting positive activity as soon as the storm starts, perhaps with treats or a favorite toy. Turn on some soothing music or white noise. Sometimes you can desensitize your Peke during calm weather using thunderstorm CDs at low volume while plying him with treats and affection. Increase the volume, getting to the loud booming sounds over a period of weeks.

Several companies have come out with jackets for the dogs to wear during storms. The Anxiety Wrap® uses maintained pressure and acupressure to relieve stress and end/lessen fears and anxieties in dogs. The Thunder Shirt™ also uses gentle constant pressure for a calming effect.

Chapter 8

Activities With Your Pekingese

There is nothing better than hanging out with your dog—unless it is sharing fun activities with him! Although the Pekingese is not considered the most athletic of his canine family, you should never underestimate his potential. Just realize that this breed is very sensitive to heat and often lacks the stamina of other breeds, and adjust your activity program to meet these needs.

Before we talk about all the great things you can do together, let's explore the best way to transport your Peke to these activities.

Traveling With Your Pekingese

Most dogs love to travel, whether it is by car or stroller. The Pekingese is a very portable dog and easy to transport. Even crates and bags designed for traveling with toy dogs are small and lightweight.

By Car

A well-ventilated crate or dog airline bag is the safest way to transport your Peke by car. A canine car seat (some of which attach to the car's seat belt) will work as long as it totally restrains your dog. In case of an accident, it will prevent him from being thrown from the car or running away. Although you might be tempted, it is not safe to hold a dog on your lap in the car. This is especially true when you are in a seat protected by air bags. If your car

has front-seat air bags, the safest place for your dog is secured in the back seat.

Car window shades near your dog's spot in the car help keep the area cool. Of course, never leave your dog in the car when it is warm outside. It takes only minutes for a dog to die of heatstroke or suffocation—and the Pekingese is particularly susceptible to these problems. If there is no way around leaving your pet in the car, leave him at home.

If your dog has a tendency to become carsick, ask your vet about anti-nausea medication. Don't feed him the morning of the trip, but you can give him a little bit of water.

For longer trips, take along food and water and some basic grooming tools. Some "waterless shampoo" could also come in handy, as will your dog's favorite toys when he starts to get bored.

Make provisions for picking up poop at rest stops; use sandwich bags or other plastic bags and dispose of them properly. During flea season, it doesn't hurt to have some flea spray with you to spray your dog before you take him for a walk. Spritz his crate before you put him back in as well, in case any wayward fleas jump off.

Attach information about your dog to his crate, in case of an accident. Include your name, address, phone numbers, and e-mail address, and any pertinent medical information about the dog. In a worst-case scenario, include the information of a contact person who can speak for your dog if you are unable to.

By Air

A Pekingese is small enough to go on board with you in an airline-approved carry-on bag. Have his collar and leash easily accessible for walking prior to departure. Also make sure he is wearing his identification tags and is microchipped. Tape important information on his travel kennel, including his name, home address, phone numbers, and any essential medications.

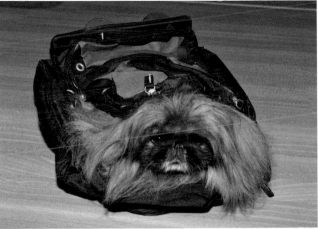
A Pekingese is small enough to go on the plane with you in an airline-approved carry-on bag.

Don't sedate your Peke because this can affect his respiratory and/or cardiovascular function at high altitudes. It will also affect his ability to maintain equilibrium if he is jostled around. Some airlines will not accept sedated pets at all.

Avoid having your Peke travel in cargo! With the problems Pekingese can have with heat exhaustion and breathing, that can be very risky. If there is no other option, take him to an airport where he can get a direct flight to his destination so that (1) he won't have to sit on the tarmac or in an unfamiliar airport waiting to change planes, and (2) a mix-up in flights can't occur. Make sure the cargo area of the plane is 100 percent pressurized!

Check with your airline about its vaccination and health certificate policy. If you are flying out of the country, keep in mind that many rabies-free countries have a quarantine period. Some airlines have restrictions on how many dogs are allowed in the cabin at a time, so make reservations early. There is a lot to check on when preparing to fly with your dog! Check the Federal Aviation Administration's (FAA) website (www.faa.gov) for complete regulations.

Lodging

More and more motels and other lodging facilities are allowing pets to stay. Some require a damage deposit, which may or may not be refundable. Be sure to keep your Peke in his crate while you are out of the room so that he will be safe when the housekeeping staff comes to clean. Put plastic under the crate and have carpet spray for cleanup, just in case. Try to avoid leaving your dog alone, even in the crate, if he will bark. This could create a nuisance and get you thrown out of your room, and it also indicates your dog is stressed or afraid.

Pet Sitters

Pet sitters are the ultimate alternative to taking your dog on a trip. These professionals stay at your house while you are away or come in several times per day to take care of your dog. Pets are happier and less stressed at home, and their exposure to illness is minimized.

Pet sitters are the ultimate alternative to taking your dog on a trip.

Some pet sitters offer services such as dog walking, pooper-scooping, and errand services. If you are unable to run your dog to the vet, your dog sitter can help out there as well. Typically, the pet sitter will become an invaluable member of the family.

Events to Share With Your Pekingese

There are many activities you can share with your Peke, including competing in dog shows, visiting nursing homes, and visiting classrooms to show children how to raise a good canine citizen. Many communities have kennel clubs, obedience clubs, or other canine organizations that offer fun activities for the public.

Conformation (Dog Shows)

The world of conformation showing may be of interest to you. American Kennel Club (AKC) dog shows draw more than three million entries annually. In conformation events, the judge examines each dog to see whether the teeth, muscles, bones, and coat texture conform to the breed's standard. The judge views each dog in profile for overall balance and watches each dog move to see how all of those features fit together in action. The dogs do not actually compete against each other. They are judged by how closely they meet the standard for the breed. The closer your dog is to the breed standard, the better chance he will have of doing well. Championship titles are earned at conformation events.

There are several types of conformation shows.

- All-breed: These competitions are for more than 150 breeds and varieties of dogs recognized by the AKC.
- Group: These shows are limited to dogs belonging to one of the seven AKC groups: Herding, Hound, Non-Sporting, Sporting, Terrier, Toy (which includes Pekingese), and Working.
- Specialty: Specialty shows are restricted to dogs of a specific breed, such as the one held annually by the Pekingese Club of America (PCA) and shows held by regional Pekingese clubs.

In order to be eligible to compete, your Peke must be at least six months old and AKC registered (but not on a Limited Registration). Spayed or neutered dogs are not eligible to compete in conformation classes.

If you have children, Junior Showmanship may be a fun activity. Offered for children 9 to 18 years of age, juniors are judged on how skillfully they present their dogs rather than on the dog

In conformation, dogs are judged by how closely they meet the standard for the breed.

himself. Many kennel clubs teach junior showmanship classes, or your child can enroll in a class for adults.

Check out the AKC's website (www.akc. org) to see what shows are coming up in your area.

Going to a Dog Show

If you decide to attend (but not exhibit at) a dog show, the AKC offers these suggestions, and I paraphrase:

- Do not take your Peke with you. Dogs who are not entered in the show typically are not allowed on the premises.
- Do not pet a dog without asking for permission from the owner or handler. The dog may be groomed and ready to go into the show ring, and you wouldn't

SPORTS AND SAFETY

Because of their short noses, Pekingese may suffer from breathing difficulties and be more prone to heatstroke. Take extra care in hot weather when exercising and when traveling. Provide plenty of cool water and shade. A spray bottle filled with water can be used to lightly mist your Peke's tummy and face if he has a short coat. Take along frozen gel packs for him to lie on to keep cool.

If you observe signs of heatstroke, such as excessive salivation and panting, diarrhea, vomiting, and even collapse, get veterinary assistance immediately! While awaiting help, cover him with a towel saturated with room-temperature water and put him in front of a fan to expedite cooling. Spray his pads with alcohol mixed with water and use those gel packs!

---

want to mess up the dog's perfect look.

- Seating is usually limited, so bring a chair with you or arrive early enough to get a seat.
- Visit the information booths for tips and advice on nutrition, grooming, health, etc. And don't forget to visit the vendors to buy a cool new toy for your Peke!
- If you are considering getting a purebred dog, this is an excellent place to do your research. Talk to the breeders and exhibitors, since they are the experts on the breed. Approach them only after they have finished showing, however, because beforehand they will be concentrating on getting to the ring.
- Shows prone to crowded conditions at ringside often prohibit baby strollers. This protects the dogs from being bumped. If you take your young child, be careful that she does not grab or poke the dogs within reach.

Another bit of advice—be courteous with your cell phones and other devices around the show grounds, especially outside the rings. The noises could be distracting to a dog and break his concentration, ruining his time in the spotlight.

Companion Events

There are not many Pekingese in companion sports, but those who do participate often surprise people by their willingness to learn and ability to excel. If your Peke has a desire to please you and you are able to maximize his willingness to learn, he can compete with the best of the obedience breeds.

The American Kennel Club offers a variety of companion events. You and your Peke can compete in obedience, agility, rally, and tracking. Unlike showing, a dog does not have to be "conformation" quality, can be spayed or neutered, and does not have to be in show coat in order to participate—he just has to have fun.

Many kennel clubs, obedience clubs, and individuals offer classes that help you train your dog and understand the regulations that apply when you are competing. With an understanding trainer, support, and verbal connection, you and your Peke can enjoy hours of fun and satisfaction.

The AKC has downloadable pamphlets about all of the organization's activities. It is best to keep current with them because things change as dog sports grow.

A note of caution: The following activities require varying degrees of running and jumping. Most Peke handlers limit their entries in these events to air-conditioned buildings, or if outside, to when the weather is much cooler. Even grass that is not freshly trimmed can be high enough to make walking or running more strenuous for the Peke. The Pekingese is simply unable to endure the exercise most other breeds can endure to compete in these events. Even in cooler venues, the handlers take ice packs and other items we have talked about to ensure that the dog stays cool.

Agility

Agility is the fastest-growing dog sport in the United States. The dog demonstrates his versatility by following cues from the handler through a timed obstacle course of jumps, tunnels, weave poles, and other objects. This activity provides fun and exercise for both dog and handler, not to mention fun for the spectators!

A dog must earn three qualifying scores under two different judges for a title. The minimum time allowed to run the course and the number of obstacles to complete successfully increase as the level of difficulty increases. There are three levels for each class: Novice, Open, and Excellent. In the Excellent B level the dog/handler teams can earn the title of Master Agility Champion (MACH).

Obedience

Obedience trials in the United States date back to 1933. The original concept was to develop a close working relationship between humans and dogs and demonstrate the usefulness and enthusiasm of dogs. Trials have become much more specific since then, but this concept remains important today.

At an obedience trial, the dog and his handler (you) are judged on how closely the two of you match the judge's mental picture of a theoretically perfect performance. There are three levels of obedience. Novice includes heel, stand for exam, figure 8, recall, long sit, and long down. Open includes the same exercises as Novice, plus drop on

PUPPY MANNERS

Whether your puppy is greeting guests in his home or making a public appearance, he needs to demonstrate manners to show he is as aristocratic as he looks! Start your puppy out right by teaching him basic commands such as *sit, stay, heel*, and *come*. Using praise is the best method of training, but treats work well also.

recall, retrieve, high jump, and broad jump, adjusted to breed requirements. Utility level tests the dog's skills even further with signal exercises, scent discrimination, and directed retrieve of an object.

Each time a dog receives a qualifying score, he earns a "leg." The dog must earn three legs for a title, such as Companion Dog (CD), Companion Dog Excellent (CDX), Utility Dog (UD), and Utility Dog Excellent (UDX). More advanced dogs and handlers can go on to an Obedience Trial Championship (OTCH) and the National Obedience Champion (NOC).

By the way—the person handling the dog is judged just as much as the dog is. Handler errors are penalized as much as any mistakes the dog makes.

Rally (Rally Obedience)

In rally, the dog and handler team completes a course of tasks that has been designed by a judge. The team moves at its own pace, very similar to rally-style auto racing. The judge tells the team to

begin, and the team moves at a brisk but normal pace with the dog under control at the handler's left side, reaching sign posts where they will be asked to perform tasks such as *sit, stay, down, come*, and *heel* position. At advanced levels, at least one jump is added and the work is done off leash. The judge watches for a smooth performance as well as skill in following the directions at each station. Scoring is not as strict as in traditional obedience.

Teamwork between the dog and handler is essential. Handlers are allowed to talk, praise, encourage, clap their hands, pat their legs, or use any verbal means of encouragement (except in Rally Excellent and Rally Advanced Excellent, where the handler is not allowed to clap her hands or pat her leg). Each performance is timed, but times are counted only if two dogs earn the same score. There are three levels: Novice, Advanced, and Excellent. Titles are Rally Novice (RN), Rally Advanced (RA), Rally Excellent (RE), and Rally Advanced Excellent (RAE).

This sport was designed with the

traditional pet owner in mind, but it can also be enjoyed at higher levels of competition.

Tracking

As of this writing, there have been no Pekingese awarded a title in tracking. Just in case you want your dog to be the first, here is a little bit about the sport.

In this event, the dog is totally in charge. The test is designed to evaluate his ability to follow a trail by finding articles left on the track. The handler must show all the articles to the judges at the end of the track. If he succeeds, he earns the tracking title for that level.

A dog can earn three AKC Tracking titles, each with an increased degree of difficulty: the Tracking Dog (TD) title, the Tracking Dog Excellent (TDX), and the Variable Surface Tracker (VST) title. Champion Tracker (CT), a very elite title, is awarded only to those dogs who have earned all three tracking titles.

Registration for Events

To compete in the events listed above, your Peke must be registered with the AKC, with either a full or a Limited Registration. The latter is a stipulation set by your dog's breeder and means the dog is registered but that no litters produced by that dog are eligible for registration. Limited Registration dogs can compete in all events except conformation, where a full AKC registration is required.

Rally was designed with the traditional pet owner in mind, but it can also be enjoyed at higher levels of competition.

Ask the Expert

Q: What's a good way to spend more time with my Pekingese?

A: "Rally is a great place to start. Rally offers the novice a supportive and encouraging network of fellow trainers. It is designed for constant communication between handler and dog during exercises, an integral part of keeping a Peke engaged in the current activity. With an understanding trainer, support, and verbal connection, you can enjoy hours of fun and satisfaction.

"Or when ready, you and your Peke can enter the show ring. The small fluffy Pekingese stands out among the Working, Sporting, Herding, and Toy breeds, bringing smiles to the faces of judges and spectators alike."

—Pat D'Arcy, Pekingese trainer and exhibitor

If you have a rescued or unregistered Peke, make note that dogs of any AKC-recognized breed may qualify for a Purebred Alternative Listing/Indefinite Listing Privilege (PAL/ILP). This makes them eligible to participate in performance events. Photos are required to prove a dog is of a registrable breed. The dog must be spayed or neutered.

The AKC Canine Partners program now allows mixed-breed dogs or dogs ineligible for AKC registration to compete in events such as obedience, rally, and agility. These dogs also must be spayed or neutered. So even a Pekingese mix can now compete!

Other Activities

While competition can be fun for many people, it may not be for you. Luckily, there are still plenty of fun and rewarding things you can do with your Peke. Here are just a few you might want to try.

Canine Good Citizen® Program

The AKC's Canine Good Citizen (CGC) Program rewards dogs with good manners at home and in the community. Often kennel clubs and obedience clubs will give the CGC test in conjunction with conformation shows and matches, or at special club events. The test includes:

• Accepting a friendly stranger
• Appearance and grooming
• Coming when called
• Reaction to another dog
• Reaction to distraction
• *Sit* and *down* commands, and staying in place (*stay*)
• Sitting politely for petting

- Supervised separation
- Walking on a loose leash
- Walking through a crowd

These items are all performed on leash. You may encourage, praise, and even pet the dog between exercises, but you cannot use food, treats, or squeaky toys. Any dog who shows "bad citizenship" like growling, snapping, biting, or attempting to attack a person or another dog is dismissed from the test. If your dog passes the test he'll receive a certificate from the AKC and will be recorded in the Canine Good Citizen Archive.

A dog who has passed the CGC test will enjoy many benefits in life. He has a greater likelihood of being accepted as a therapy or service dog, and he can be more easily trained for AKC performance events. A rental agency that normally will not rent to people with dogs may waive that stipulation if your Peke has passed the test.

Service Dogs

The most well-known type of service dog is the Seeing Eye dog, an occupation reserved for larger dog breeds. However, there are other services a small dog like a Pekingese can provide, such as being trained to assist people with varying degrees of hearing impairment. The dogs alert their owner to sounds such as a doorbell, phone, smoke alarm, or a crying baby. Some service dogs alert the owner if their insulin levels are low or if an epileptic seizure is imminent.

In the United States, service dogs are legally defined by the Americans With Disabilities Act (ADA) and are trained to do work or perform tasks for the benefit of a person with a disability. Federal laws protect the rights of individuals with disabilities to be accompanied by their service animals in public places. Service animals are not considered pets, but the owners are known to give them playtime when not working.

Therapy Dogs

Therapy dogs visit hospitals, nursing homes, and other institutions in order to bring love and comfort to those in need. Therapy animals are not defined by federal law, but some states have laws defining therapy animals. You may be able to have your Peke certified as a therapy dog locally, or you can work with national organizations. The two national organizations that stand out in the area of therapy animals are Therapy Dogs International (TDI) and Pet Partners, a program of the Delta Society.

Therapy Dogs International (TDI) is dedicated to regulating, testing, and registering therapy dogs and their volunteer handlers for the purpose of visiting nursing homes, hospitals, and wherever else therapy dogs are needed. TDI has registered more than 21,000 dog/

handler teams since being founded in 1976.

TDI activities include:

- Tail Waggin' Tutors, a "Children Reading to Dogs" program, has shown that reading to dogs increases children's self-esteem and nurtures an interest in reading.
- Disaster Relief attends to the emotional needs of displaced persons, family members, and relief workers.
- Bereavement services incorporate therapy dogs in providing consolation to family members.

For more information on how you and your Peke can become a TDI team, visit www.tdi-dog.org.

Pet Partners helps people live healthier and happier lives by incorporating therapy, service, and companion animals into their lives. Activities include:

- The Pet Partners program trains and screens volunteers with their pets so that they can visit patients/clients in hospitals, nursing homes, hospice, schools, and many other facilities.
- Pet loss and bereavement services provide resources for people who have lost an animal companion.

A well-trained Peke can make a wonderful therapy dog.

OUT AND ABOUT WITH YOUR PEKE

✓ Transport your Peke in a well-ventilated crate or airline bag.

✓ Make every effort to take him on board with you when flying, rather than shipping him in cargo, where he may have breathing difficulties.

✓ Consider a pet sitter when you can't take your Peke with you.

✓ Attend a dog show to see what activities you can do together.

✓ Get your Peke certified as a Canine Good Citizen.

✓ Become a therapy dog team with your Peke.

Find out more by visiting the Pet Partners website at www.petpartnersusa.com.

There are a lot of local programs for therapy dogs, too. Some libraries have their own Children Reading to Dogs programs, and often dog clubs organize visitations to schools or nursing homes. Check with your local clubs to see what they have organized.

A number of Pekes are certified as therapy dogs and do very well. Their size makes them portable and small enough to fit on laps or on the side of a bed. As a friend told me, "They are small, soft little wind-up toys that put smiles on people's faces. Their loving yet clown-like personalities make them the ideal visitor for someone who needs a boost."

Chapter
9

Health of Your
Pekingese

In the endearing novel *All Creatures Great and Small*, British veterinarian James Herriot quotes an overanxious Pekingese owner as saying, "Oh, Mr. Herriot… Tricki has gone flop-bott again!" Flop-bott turns out to be a chronic anal gland impaction that Herriot remedies from time to time.

Since the publication of this book in 1972, veterinary medicine has grown at a miraculously fast pace. Pets are living longer and better, and pet owners have become more educated in how to care for their animals without panicking about flop-bott!

Finding a Veterinarian

Finding a capable and caring veterinarian is one of the first things you should do for your Peke. Ask your friends and family members about their experiences with clinics in the area. Take time to select the clinic you feel the most comfortable with. After all, this will be a very important partnership during the life of your new companion.

Before you make your first appointment, stop by the clinic to get an overall feel of the facilities.

- Is the space clean, modern, and well organized?
- Is the waiting room overcrowded?
- How do staff members interact with you?
- Does the hospital accept pet insurance policies?
- Will the office hours work with your schedule?
- Are overnight patients monitored?
- Do they have after-hours emergency coverage, either at the clinic or at another facility?
- Are the doctors members of a professional veterinary association?

If you are transferring from one clinic to another, be sure to ask for a complete copy of your dog's health records to be sent to your new vet.

First Vet Visit

The first visit to the veterinarian should be a pleasant experience, since there will be more in the future. If your dog is accustomed to being handled, it will be easier for the vet to conduct the exam. Take along your Peke's favorite treats or a toy to distract him, and praise him when he is good. If your vet is rough with your dog and makes him fearful, consider changing clinics. Going for medical procedures is a fact of life, and your Peke should not feel uncomfortable. Take him along with you to the vet's office when you go to pick up medications, where he can just go in, hang out, and leave so that he won't always associate the clinic with treatments.

The other animals in the waiting room should be restrained. Other dogs may be ill or aggressive, so you will want to keep your Peke in your lap or take

PUPPY'S FIRST EXAM

Schedule your Peke's first exam as soon as possible to make sure his health and temperament are sound. Until his vaccinations are complete, take him into the clinic in his carrier to minimize exposure to germs. Find out what preventive measures are needed based on the health concerns in your community, and ask about medical issues unique to the Pekingese. After the exam, let your Peke's breeder know whether there were any problems. A reputable breeder will stand behind the guarantee of a healthy puppy.

him in his carrier. Until he has had his vaccinations, one option is to check in with the veterinary staff and stay in the car with your dog until it's time for the actual appointment. Then carry him straight into the exam room. A staff member can wave you in or even ring you on your cell phone.

Annual Vet Visit

The best gift you can give your Peke on his birthday—well, maybe a few days after his birthday—is an annual examination, more often for an older dog or one with a chronic illness. The annual exam gives your vet an opportunity to:

- Give any needed vaccinations
- Check a stool sample for parasites
- Do a blood test for heartworms
- Determine whether your dog is in good weight and has good muscle tone
- Observe any coat or skin problems, such as change in pigment, shedding, or lumps

- Measure heart rate and listen to the lungs
- Check his mouth for gum disease, tooth decay, tumors, etc.
- Check the ears for infections or discharge
- Check the eyes for discharge, cloudiness, glaucoma, or Peke-related eye disease

Point out anything unusual you have noticed. Has he been having accidents in the house? Is he drinking more water or not finishing his food? Even seemingly insignificant behavior such as excess belching, passing gas, unusual stools, resisting exercise, or sneezing could be significant. Has there been any discharge from his eyes or nose? Change in temperament may also have a medical origin.

Let your vet know about any supplements, special diets, or alternative medicine treatments your Peke is receiving. If you have seen another vet or made any emergency visits, take those medical records with you so that your vet will have a complete history.

Your vet will probably want to do a routine test called a CBC (complete blood count). This test, which checks the number and types of blood cells present, can diagnose disorders such as infections, diabetes, autoimmune diseases, and anemia. The test can point to the early stages of renal failure or liver disease. Other tests may be in order based on the examination.

Don't be afraid to express any concerns you may have, whether it is financial or about a medical procedure. It is better that your vet understand your concerns to be able to help you with options.

Vaccinations

Newborn puppies receive antibodies through their mother's milk. After your puppy is weaned he needs vaccinations to help his body form new antibodies against disease. The breeder should provide you with a record of any vaccinations your puppy has had so that your vet will know how to proceed.

With at least 14 different vaccines available, not all dogs should be vaccinated with all vaccines. For example, there are areas in the United States that may have a heavy incidence

The best gift you can give your Peke for his birthday is an annual vet examination.

of Lyme disease, while others may have very few cases. Your vet will consider all the risk factors in order to customize a vaccination program for your Peke. Let her know whether your dog will be in contact with other dogs, such as at kennels, obedience classes, or dog parks because these factors will impact your dog's risk of exposure to certain diseases. Make sure your vet is aware of any previous adverse reactions to vaccines.

Core Vaccines

The four core vaccinations include those against canine distemper, canine hepatitis, parvovirus, and rabies.

Canine Distemper

Canine distemper is caused by a virus similar to the one that causes measles in people. The virus attacks the central nervous system. Signs appear six to nine days after exposure and can range from fever, loss of appetite, and listlessness to seizures and death. This highly contagious disease is airborne, and infected animals shed the virus in all body secretions. Dogs can recover from distemper, but permanent brain damage can result.

Canine Hepatitis

Canine hepatitis is caused by a virus called canine adenovirus, spread through the urine and feces of infected dogs. If not treated quickly, this disease can kill puppies in a matter of hours, even before you see symptoms. Symptoms include fever, loss of appetite, lethargy, runny eyes and nose, and in later stages, bleeding under the skin, jaundice (yellowing of skin), and bluish clouding of the eyes. If your dog recovers, he will be more vulnerable to kidney infections and may suffer serious permanent damage to his liver and eyesight.

Parvovirus

Parvovirus is spread through contact with infected feces. The causative organism can live on inanimate surfaces, making it difficult to stop from spreading. Signs are vomiting, very putrid diarrhea, dehydration, dark or bloody feces, and in severe cases, fever and lowered white blood cell counts. Parvovirus is deadly and treatment is costly.

Rabies

Rabies, which is spread through the saliva of an infected animal, causes aggressive behavior, seizures, and death and can be passed to other mammals, including you! Rabies vaccines are required by law; their frequency varies from state to state.

Non-Core Vaccines

Lyme Disease

Lyme disease is caused by bacteria and is spread by ticks. Ticks become infected with the bacteria by feeding on infected

FIRST AID

The PetEducation.com website has a comprehensive list of first-aid and emergency evacuation kit items, instructions for CPR and the Heimlich maneuver, and many other first-aid tips. You can download these items as PDF files so that you can study them and have them handy if your Peke is injured.

Always remember that any first aid administered to your pet should be followed by immediate veterinary care!

Have your veterinarian's number on speed dial or right beside your own emergency numbers and on your cell phone. Another number is the Animal Poison Control Center at 888-4ANI-HELP (888-426-4435). There may be a fee for this call, but the call could save your dog's life.

---

mice and other small animals. The disease is then transmitted to dogs, cats, and people by the deer tick and several other closely related ticks. Up to 95 percent of dogs infected with the bacteria do not develop symptoms, but some will show fever, loss of appetite, swollen joints, lameness, and swollen lymph nodes.

Bordetella

Bordetella, more commonly known as "kennel cough," is a highly contagious respiratory infection affecting the airways. It is commonly contracted in situations where dogs are confined in close contact, such as kennels, shelters, and grooming salons. Stress, poor ventilation, and temperature and humidity extremes are also thought to be factors. Signs are a hacking dry cough, sometimes described as a goose honk, gagging, and expulsion

of white foamy fluid. Typically, this disease is not serious, but some dogs do become very ill from the virus.

Vaccine Protocols

For many years, standard veterinary protocol called for dogs to receive annual vaccinations. Now there is increasing evidence that some vaccines provide protection beyond one year, while others may fail to protect for a full year. So one vaccination schedule will not work well for all dogs. That's why it is important to talk to your vet about personalizing a vaccination schedule for your Peke.

Studies have shown a link between vaccinations and autoimmune diseases, anemia, platelet problems, and joint disease. This is truly an area of veterinary medicine to watch. If you have a concern about overvaccinating, an antibody titer (blood test) can measure whether your dog is protected from a certain disease. Titers don't replace a vaccination program, but in some cases they may help your vet determine whether your dog really needs that vaccine.

Additionally, a puppy or a dog whose immune system is compromised or stressed by illness or a surgical procedure probably should not be vaccinated. He will not be able to develop the necessary immunities.

Vaccines can occasionally cause side effects. Compared to the risk of not vaccinating, the risk of a reaction is small in comparison. It still doesn't hurt to be familiar with the most common side effects just in case:

- Mild cough (from the intranasal bordetella and/or parainfluenza vaccine)
- Mild fever
- Decreased appetite
- Depression
- Pain, swelling, or redness at the injection site or on the dog's face

One not so common side effect, anaphylaxis, may cause shock, respiratory failure, or cardiac arrest—and death if not treated. It usually occurs within minutes to hours of the vaccination. It is very rare—about one case in every 15,000 doses administered. If you observe diarrhea, vomiting, pale gums, cold limbs, fast heart rate, weak pulse, facial swelling, seizures, and/or shock, get emergency help immediately! The dog needs a shot of epinephrine, followed by oxygen, intravenous fluids, and possibly other treatment.

As an added precaution, make your vaccination appointment for early in the morning so that you can watch your Peke throughout the day while the clinic is still open.

Internal Parasites

Heartworms are dangerous internal parasites that live in an animal's heart. Other worms live in the intestinal tract, robbing your dog of nutrients.

Heartworms

Heartworms, which are spread by mosquitoes and live in the right side of the heart, are by far the most dangerous parasites. And the treatment is the most extensive and costly. Fortunately, it is also the easiest parasite to guard against.

Some dogs don't show any signs of disease, while some show decreased appetite, loss of weight, and listlessness. Often the first sign of disease is a cough or fatigue during exercise. Some will accumulate fluid in the abdomen, making them look potbellied.

The best way to prevent heartworm infection is to give your Peke preventive medications, get annual heartworm testing (blood test), and reduce exposure to mosquitoes. A number of monthly heartworm preventives are available; some will even control other parasites.

Hookworms

Hookworms are small parasites that attach to the intestinal wall and feed on blood. The parasitical infection is often passed from the mother to the puppies, but adults can get them from infested soil. Symptoms include diarrhea that may be black and tarry from digested blood. Hookworms are not visible in fecal material but can be detected under the microscope in a routine check of a stool sample. There are a number of medications that can be used to treat hookworms, so your vet will have to help you choose the right one.

Roundworms

Roundworms are most common in puppies because they often get them from their mother, but a dog of any age can become infected. Puppies infected with large numbers of worms often have trouble gaining weight and may have "potbellies" and a dull hair coat. Sometimes coiled-up white worms are seen in a dog's vomit or feces. The type of medication and the number of treatments necessary will depend on the age of the dog and the situation, and will be determined by your vet.

Tapeworms

Tapeworms are long, segmented white worms. The head of the worm embeds

Your vet will be able to treat internal parasites.

itself into the lining of the digestive tract, with the rest of the worm trailing downstream, absorbing nutrients that pass by. Segments containing egg packets break off the worm's body and are deposited outside with the feces, or you may find them stuck on your Peke's anal area. They are shaped like grains of rice. Dogs can become infected by eating fleas that contain immature tapeworms. Sometimes your dog may show no signs, but vomiting and diarrhea can develop.

Most worms are diagnosed from a fecal sample under the microscope. Tapeworms often fail to show up in a sample, so that the best way to find them is by observation. Be sure to take along a stool sample so that the vet will not have to extract a sample from the dog (very uncomfortable for him)! Treatment for these parasites is simple and inexpensive.

Whipworms

Whipworms get their name from their long, slender bodies that are capped with a small club-like end. These worms lie coiled within the wall and lining of the large intestine. Dogs become infected by ingesting food or water contaminated with whipworm eggs. The most common sign is diarrhea with red blood. Whipworms, which can be detected under the microscope, are resistant to some of the common dewormers, so your vet will have to help you with treatment.

Other Parasites

Other less common parasites include coccidia and giardia, one-celled organisms that live in the intestinal tract. They usually affect puppies or adults whose immune system is suppressed or who are particularly stressed. Signs are weight loss and lack of appetite. Both parasitic infections can be successfully treated.

External Parasites
Fleas

Fleas are the bane of a dog owner's existence. There are more than 2,000 species of fleas, but it is *Ctenocephalides canis*, the common dog flea, that is our enemy! Besides carrying tapeworms, fleas also cause your dog nonstop scratching. It is easy to imagine how many fleas can be harbored in a Peke's thick coat, not to mention the distress they cause him. For every flea you see on your Peke, there are likely to be hundreds of eggs and larvae in your home and yard.

A number of sprays, dips, shampoos, and topicals are on the market for mild flea problems. Flea combs (32 teeth/inch) are great for grabbing them out of the coat, especially around the face. Place the fleas you comb off in detergent water to kill them.

If you plan to use strong flea dips or other over-the-counter products, it is best to ask your vet's advice because the

Peke is a toy breed and may need smaller dosages than the package says. His overall health also has to be considered. If the flea bites on your Peke are severe, you should take him to the vet. Flea bites can actually cause anemia if they draw too much blood.

In order to fight this menace, you must treat the environment as well as your dog. This involves killing the adult fleas and keeping immature fleas from developing. Here are some suggestions to eradicate adult and immature fleas.

- Vacuum the house thoroughly. Seal and discard the vacuum cleaner bag immediately. Using a carpet powder before vacuuming can be helpful, but be sure your Peke does not inhale the powder.

Check your Peke for fleas and ticks after he's been outside.

- Wash your Peke's bedding often in hot water.
- Treat your vehicle and pet carrier if you have transported him since the flea infestation.
- Don't use a flea collar on a young puppy, an elderly dog, or one who is ill. The chemicals could be harmful. They are unlikely to help with that thick coat anyway.
- Foggers can be helpful for hard-to-reach areas, but keep in mind that all living creatures must be removed from the area for the specified period of time. Read the label to see whether any of your material objects could be damaged by the spray.
- It takes persistently cold overnight temperatures to reduce the flea population outside.

Pekingese, like any other breed, can develop an allergy to fleas (flea allergy dermatitis). It only takes one flea bite to wreak havoc on that thick coat as your dog itches and scratches to no end. Your vet can treat the occasional allergic reaction with antihistamines and cortisone injections or tablets. Over-the-counter topical creams can soothe irritated skin. The best way to handle this problem is prevention!

Ticks

There are more than 500 species of ticks worldwide. These parasitic arthropods,

Q : What is the most common medical emergency in the Pekingese?

A : "The large, prominent eyes of the Pekingese make them susceptible to eye ulcers. Sometimes the facial fold can rub against the eye, or he can injure the eye in play or by rubbing against furniture. Pekes are prone to dry eye (a lack of protective tears), making it more likely an ulcer can form. Corneal ulcers are quite painful and they itch, causing your Peke to squint and rub the affected eye.

"Because of the potential to permanently impair vision or perforate the eye, a corneal ulcer is considered a medical emergency. It is more difficult to heal the ulcers because the eyes aren't as well protected by the eyelids, but they can be healed with medication. Deeper ulcers will require more aggressive treatment."

—Dr. Kristen L. King, DVM, Stonecrest Animal
Medical Center, Huntington, West Virginia

closely related to mites, attach to your dog by inserting their mouth barb into your dog's skin; they become larger as they gorge themselves on blood. Tick-transmitted diseases include Lyme disease, Rocky Mountain spotted fever, anemia, and tick bite paralysis. The same ticks that bite dogs can cause these illnesses and others if they bite humans.

How often you see ticks depends on what region of the country you live in and the time of year. Keeping your Peke and other household pets out of the grass and woods helps reduce their exposure. Perform a "tick check" on yourself and your pets after returning from outside.

Products that kill and repel ticks include once-a-month topical products, sprays, powders, dips, shampoos, and collars. There are some EPA-approved lawn and garden insecticides that can be applied under shrubs, under bushes, in crawl spaces, and along fence lines to control fleas and ticks outside. Just make sure your Peke does not inhale any of these chemicals. Keep him away from any sprays for at least four hours after application.

If your Peke is bitten by a tick, removal is tricky but possible.

- Using fine-tipped tweezers, grab the tick by the head right where it has entered the skin. Do not grasp the tick by the body.
- Pull firmly and steadily directly outward. Do not twist the tick as you are pulling.
- Place the tick in a jar of alcohol to kill it.

- Clean the bite wound with disinfectant and wash your hands thoroughly.
- The tick's head rarely stays in. Any skin irritation is due to a reaction to the tick saliva.

Breed-Specific Illnesses

The Pekingese is considered a brachycephalic breed. "Brachy" means "shortened" and "cephalic" means "head." With the gradual shortening of the muzzle over the centuries, the face and nose bones have become shortened, making the head's soft tissues not proportionate to the shortened skull.

For centuries Pekingese have lived perfectly happy and healthy lives with their unique head structure. However, when certain signs are present, medical problems can occur.

Brachycephalic Airway Syndrome (BAS)

Brachycephalic airway syndrome includes a variety of conditions resulting from the anatomy of the Pekingese head. Obesity will make these problems worse, as will a heavy facial wrinkle. BAS is considered an inherited condition.

Some Pekingese are born with stenotic nares, nostrils that are narrow or collapse inward while the dog is breathing. This condition makes him pant heavily in order to get enough oxygen. He will not be able to tolerate exercise and is at risk for heatstroke. If severe, stenotic nares can be repaired surgically to allow better airflow through the nose.

Elongated soft palate occurs where the roof of the mouth is so long that the rear tip of it protrudes into the airway and interferes with the dog's inhaling air into the lungs. Signs are noisy breathing, snorting, exercise intolerance, and blue tongue and gums from lack of oxygen. Overactivity, excitement, or excessive heat or humidity can make it worse. During sleep, the throat muscles can actually relax and impair breathing even more. Diagnosis is made by X-rays and by examining the dog under anesthesia. Treatment is surgery to trim the soft palate.

Another complication is everted laryngeal saccules, in which two small pieces of fleshy tissue in the larynx (voice box) enlarge and partially obstruct airflow. The dog creates more pressure when he inhales in order to fill his lungs with air. These sacs can be surgically removed.

A common procedure called a rhinoplasty can be performed to enlarge the nostrils and increase airflow. Other problems related to BAS can be corrected at the same time. Some vets believe that if the nares are enlarged early in life (three to four months of age), the other problems can be prevented later on.

Pekingese are sensitive to anesthesia, so be sure to discuss options with your vet before any surgery.

Overheating is especially dangerous for the Pekingese because panting causes more swelling and narrowing of the airway, increasing his anxiety. Dogs who are overweight or who live with smokers may be more at risk for these conditions.

The Eyes Have It

The shape of the Pekingese eye is a far cry from the deep and protective eye socket of his ancestor, the wolf. This shallow socket can create several problems.

Distichiasis

Distichiasis is an eye problem in which small eyelashes grow on the inner surface or very edge of the eyelids. The hairs irritate the cornea, making the eye red and inflamed and possibly causing a discharge. The dog will squint or blink often or rub the eye. In severe cases, the cornea may become ulcerated and appear bluish in color. Blindness can result if infections develop. The abnormal eyelashes should be removed surgically or by a procedure where a fine needle is passed into the hair follicle and an electric current destroys the hair and its roots. Both procedures require anesthesia.

Keratoconjunctivitis Sicca

Keratoconjunctivitis sicca (dry eye syndrome) is caused by inadequate tear production resulting from congenital disorders, infections, medications, or removal of the tear gland of the third eyelid (cherry eye). Signs are thick yellow discharge, redness, and rubbing at the eyes. The goal to helping this problem is to stimulate tear production, lubricate the eyes, decrease scar tissue, and prevent corneal ulcers and vision loss.

Proptosed Eye

Proptosed eye is literally the displacement of the eyeball out of the eye socket, producing the effect that the eyelids are trapped behind the globe. Yes, it's scary! Proptosis typically occurs following trauma to the face or head, as from a dog fight or even from picking your Peke up by the scruff of the neck. (Never do that!)

The shallow socket of the Peke's eye can cause problems.

Proptosis is considered a true eye emergency. With the lids unable to cover the eye, the surface of the eye rapidly becomes dry and discolored. A proptosed eye can result in blindness, or in extreme cases, eye loss. (Note: The eye will not fall out…it remains connected via the eye muscle.)

Superficial Pigmentary Keratitis

Superficial pigmentary keratitis occurs when irritation causes the eye to produce excess pigment as a protective measure. If this pigment extends to the cornea, it will result in vision loss. Treatment includes

If you notice a change in your Peke's behavior, take him to the vet for a checkup.

tear replacement drops, corticosteroids, and occasionally surgery. For daily eye cleaning, use sterile eyewash or eye wipes.

Uveitis

Uveitis is an inflammation of the eye. Signs to watch for are cloudiness, redness, tearing, squinting, hemorrhage within the eye, and/or loss of vision. Causes include trauma, infections, and tumors. Treatment is aimed at reducing inflammation and preventing complications such as cataracts, scar tissue, retinal disease, and glaucoma.

The Pekingese Heart

Pekingese, like many other small breeds, are prone to congestive heart failure. Heart failure is the end result of various conditions, such as a weak heart muscle or leaky heart valve. Unlike a heart attack in humans, heart failure in dogs is a slow process that occurs over months or years.

Keeping your Peke healthy and at his ideal weight can lessen the severity of symptoms. Good oral health is crucial because heart valves can be injured by infection if dental problems allow bacteria from the mouth to enter the bloodstream.

In 2011, the North Carolina State University Veterinary Teaching Hospital launched a website called The Cardiology Care Network (www.

cardiologycarenetwork.com) to help people manage their pets with cardiac disease. This is a good resource for you if your Peke should develop any type of heart disease.

Orthopedic Conditions

Like many other toy breeds, Pekingese are prone to several orthopedic conditions.

Intervertebral Disk Disease

Intervertebral disk disease occurs when a portion of the intervertebral disk herniates and compresses the spinal cord. The result can be pain, weakness, stumbling, or an arched back. Pain can be managed by anti-inflammatory medications and muscle relaxers, and by keeping your Peke strictly confined, usually for about two weeks. Physical therapy or acupuncture may be prescribed.

In severe cases you will see paralysis, loss of sensation, inability to control bladder and bowels, and other severe neurological deficits. Surgery to relieve the pressure on the spinal cord is usually performed at this point. The recovery rate is highest if the surgery is performed within 48 hours. Some dogs with permanent rear limb paralysis can do well managed at home with special carts to allow them to move about.

It is vital to prevent your Peke from gaining too much weight. In addition to the other problems obesity can cause, back and joint problems can be worsened by carrying too much weight.

Patellar Luxation

Patellar luxation is basically a loose or displaced kneecap. The ridges forming the patellar (knee) groove are too shallow, causing the patella to jump out of the groove sideways. You may notice a mild to moderate lameness, or you may see your Peke stretch his leg backward in an effort to reduce the pain. Patellar luxation may be congenital or caused by trauma. You can help prevent these conditions by keeping your Peke from jumping—a hard thing to do if he loves flying off your furniture! If you can train him to use a ramp or a set of steps up to your couch or bed from puppyhood, he may be able to avoid jump-related injuries.

Pancreatitis

Pancreatitis is either acute or chronic inflammation of the pancreas. When enzymes become activated within the pancreas, they begin digesting the actual glandular tissue, causing the inflammation. In serious cases, pancreatitis can result in long-term ramifications such as diabetes.

Signs include abdominal pain, vomiting, and loss of appetite. If the pain is severe, the dog may be in a hunched position. He may also have diarrhea or stools with small amounts of fresh blood and/or mucus. Low-grade cases may not show all of the signs and may be confused with other diseases. In severe cases, the dog may become dehydrated, collapse, go into shock, and may even suffer renal shutdown and distressed breathing.

It is vital to take your Peke to the vet as soon as possible if you suspect pancreatitis. Diagnosis is made by blood tests; your vet may also recommend an X-ray to rule out other conditions. Most cases are treated with intravenous fluids, pain relief, and letting the pancreas heal on its own.

The most common risk factors for pancreatitis are obesity, especially in spayed females, a high-fat diet, and a buildup of toxins in the body. The toxins can be medications, household chemicals, and pesticides.

A low-fat, high-fiber diet is generally

The Pekingese is particularly prone to the reverse sneeze because of his shorter face and being low to the ground.

suggested to prevent further attacks. If your Peke has chronic pancreatitis, a single fatty meal can be enough to set off a bout of pancreatitis!

Reverse Sneeze (Inspiratory Paraxysmal Respiration)

Let's call it by that first term! The reverse sneeze can be terrifying the first time you hear it. Your dog will make a loud, snorting sound as he attempts to clear his nose and throat by inhaling a sneeze rather than exhaling. After you panic and wonder what could be wrong, you will remember that this display is caused by allergies, dust, cigarette smoke, or a bit of mucus—anything that causes a normal sneeze. The Pekingese is particularly prone to the reverse sneeze because of his shorter face and being low to the ground.

You don't really have to do anything when your Peke reverse sneezes because it will stop on its own. It is very hard to stand by and watch, though, so here are a few things you can try:

- Take his mind off the attack by placing your finger on his tongue or over his nose.
- Massage his throat from the jaw to the larynx.
- Blow in his nose until he stops.
- Put your fingers over his nostrils to force him to breathe through his mouth, massaging his throat if possible.

If your Peke reverse sneezes too often,

check with your vet to rule out canine nasal mites or an upper respiratory condition.

Occasionally what appears to be a reverse sneeze is something more serious. The episode could be a collapsed trachea (windpipe), an upper-airway obstruction, or a heart condition. The suggestions in the bulleted list above would likely make these conditions worse, not better, and other signs of disease would be present, such as fainting or exercise intolerance.

Jerking or tugging on your Peke's collar could actually cause damage to the trachea or larynx (voice box). This is dangerous! Handle your Peke gently— he deserves it. Use a harness to keep pressure off the throat area.

Reverse sneezing generally is a benign condition. If you are worried, have your vet rule out anything more serious. If possible, video your Peke while he is "sneezing"—you know he'll never do it while the vet is watching!

Umbilical Hernias

An umbilical hernia occurs when the umbilical ring fails to close fully after birth and abdominal contents protrude through the belly button. This loop feels like a soft mass. Umbilical hernias can be caused by heredity, cutting the umbilical cord too short, or excessive stress on the cord during delivery. They generally will be apparent by six weeks of age. A small hernia is generally not a problem. If the hernia is large, it should be repaired to prevent the loop from becoming trapped, causing a life-threatening "strangulation." Signs of intestinal strangulation are vomiting, not eating, depression, and a hernia that is warm to the touch.

Cancer

Cancer affects an estimated 50 percent of dogs over the age of ten. The Veterinary Cancer Society has identified ten common warning signs of caner:

• Abnormal swellings that persist or continue to grow
• Sores that don't heal
• Weight loss
• Loss of appetite
• Bleeding or discharge
• Offensive odor
• Difficulty swallowing or eating
• Hesitation to exercise or loss of stamina
• Persistent lameness or stiffness
• Difficulty breathing, urinating, or defecating.

Remember, these signs do not necessarily mean your Peke has cancer. They do mean something, however, and need to be investigated.

Mammary Cancer

Because estrogen is one of the primary causes of mammary cancer, a female Pekingese who is spayed before her first heat cycle has virtually no chance of getting breast cancer. The benefit decreases with each heat cycle, but some benefit has been shown even in older females. The earliest a female should be spayed is six months of age.

Give your Peke a breast exam annually and more often when she gets older. Check the entire chest area, not just the nipples. Look for small growths that feel like pea gravel and are difficult to move. Tumors grow rapidly in a short period of time.

As canine surgery goes, removing a small tumor is relatively minor because the tumor grows just under the skin. Surgery is more complicated, of course, for larger or multiple tumors. Some dogs have been successfully treated with chemotherapy if the tumor has metastasized. Radiation and hormone therapy may be available soon. Approximately 50 percent of tumors are malignant, and 25 percent prove to be fatal.

Testicular Cancer

Testicular cancer is one of the most common cancers in males, particularly older males. Castration is usually the treatment, proceeded by abdominal and/or chest X-rays to make sure the tumor has not spread. Chemotherapy may be successful if the tumor has metastasized.

If your male Peke has one or more retained testicles, it is even more important to neuter him. If you don't, he will be much more likely to develop testicular cancer.

Spaying and Neutering

Spaying Your Female Pekingese

Spaying is the removal of both ovaries and uterus. Other surgical options allow females to continue producing estrogen. A tubal ligation retains the hormone-producing ovaries. A hysterectomy removes the uterus but retains the ovaries. Canine birth control medications and hormone-replacement therapy are also being studied.

These other options are not commonly performed in veterinary medicine, and the female will still have the same disadvantages as an unspayed female. Discuss these options with your breeder

Cancer affects an estimated 50 percent of dogs over the age of ten.

SPAYING OR NEUTERING YOUR PEKE

If your female Peke is spayed before her first heat cycle, the chance that she will develop malignant mammary tumors is virtually zero. Spaying also eliminates uterine and mammary infections, very sad-to-watch false pregnancies, and unwanted real pregnancies. The earlier you neuter your male Peke, the greater chances are that he will not mark territory, develop aggressive tendencies, suffer from testicular cancer or perianal hernias, or sire an unwanted litter.

and your vet to determine what is best for your girl.

Cancer prevention is not the only reason to spay your Peke.

- Some females experience false pregnancies due to hormonal fluctuations. Their abdomens may swell, they may make nests, and they may even adopt an object as a baby (a very sad thing to watch). Milk in the mammary glands can cause mastitis (infected glands).
- Females can develop pyometra (literally, pus in the uterus). Pyometra can be life-threatening, and a female so affected will need to be spayed immediately. The surgery can be risky, as bacteria can leak to the bloodstream.
- There is always the risk of an unwanted pregnancy.
- There is no menopause in dogs. Unless spayed, females have heat cycles their entire lives.
- There is the sanitary aspect of a female in heat. Unless she is able to keep herself clean, there can be staining and odor associated with the cycle.

If you are thinking about breeding your female, consider that something could go wrong. She could have difficult labor, uterine or mammary gland infections, or eclampsia, an acute, life-threatening disease caused by low blood calcium levels. Small dogs like the Pekingese often need C-sections, which can be risky for her and add to the expense of the litter. After a C-section, which of course requires anesthesia, the mother often has difficulty bonding with her babies. That will mean more work for you keeping them clean and fed. In fact, many first-time mothers have difficulty with their babies or don't produce enough milk.

And keep in mind that puppies don't always come out all wiggly and cute and ready to nurse. Some are weak, malformed, or simply unable to survive. This information is not to scare you, but you need to be aware that a little Peke does not always have an uneventful birthing.

Neutering Your Male Pekingese

Neutering the male Pekingese is a much simpler matter. The procedure, during which both testicles are removed, is low risk and relatively inexpensive, especially for a small dog. There is some debate as to how early dogs can be neutered, but most are neutered between five and eight months of age, before unwanted behaviors have started. And your Peke doesn't care that he is neutered—honestly!

An alternative to neutering is a vasectomy, just as in humans. This procedure is not widely performed because it does not provide the same medical benefits as neutering. And he will still need to be neutered later on to prevent disease.

Aside from cancer prevention, there are other reasons to consider neutering your male:

- Unneutered males tend to mark their territory and want to roam.
- Neutering removes the more pungent odor of the urine.
- Unneutered males are more likely to be aggressive due to increased testosterone levels.
- There are fewer perineal hernias in neutered older males. A perineal hernia, which can be found in the pelvic, abdominal, or rectal area, can be very painful and requires costly surgery.
- Perineal adenomas (benign) or perineal adenocarcinomas (malignant) are very rare in neutered males, since the growth of this tumor is due to testosterone.
- More than 80 percent of unneutered males develop prostate disease due to the presence of testosterone.

Strangely enough, if you have your dog neutered he can have prosthetic testicles implanted. So if you think your male dog is really going to have an identity crisis, consider that an option!

Alternative/Holistic Therapies

Alternative and holistic medicines share this philosophy: Consider and treat all aspects of the patient's life, not just the symptoms. A holistic veterinarian will combine the best of Western medicine along with natural therapies such as

Spaying and neutering have many health benefits.

acupuncture, chiropractic, physical therapy, massage, nutrition, herbal medicine, yoga, and homeopathy. The holistic vet will look at possible causes of disease such as environmental conditions, nutritional deficiencies, or emotional stress and educate you on what to do to keep your Peke well. To find a holistic veterinarian, visit the American Holistic Veterinary Medical Association (AHVMA) at www.ahvma.org.

A holistic veterinarian will combine the best of Western medicine along with natural therapies.

Massage therapy is something you can do for your Peke—not in lieu of medical treatment but as an alternative to petting him. In a breed as solid as the Peke, you can imagine how good massage would feel to him and how much he would appreciate your attention. One good resource is *Dog Massage: A Whiskers-to-Tail Guide to Your Dog's Ultimate Petting Experience*, by licensed (human) massage therapist Maryjean Ballner.

Senior Dogs

Dogs the size of a Pekingese, that is, those under 20 pounds (9 kg), are considered seniors at 11 to 12 years of age. As your dog approaches this golden age, your vet will be checking for signs of age-related illness. This number is just a rule of thumb—some dogs will not seem old at this age, whereas others will show signs earlier.

Never assume a physical change is "just old age." Often a limp could be tendonitis;

accidents in the house could be a urinary tract infection or diabetes; an irritating lump could be a simple cyst—all of those things are treatable.

On the other hand, your senior dog is more prone to disease processes such as cancer, heart disease, and kidney disease, many of which can be managed well at home, often for long periods of time. It is best to have your vet check those signs right away so that treatment can begin immediately.

Cognitive Dysfunction

There is nothing sadder than watching your beloved Pekingese decline in health and personality. One cause is cognitive dysfunction, also known as "Doggy Alzheimer's."

A dog suffering from dementia may:
• Sleep during the day and stay awake at night
• Appear more anxious

- Have a loss of appetite
- Bark for no reason, especially at night
- Not greet you or recognize you
- Get lost in the yard or house
- Soil in the house
- Become timid or aggressive

There are several treatment options for cognitive dysfunction. Always check with your vet before using any of the over-the-counter drugs mentioned.

- A prescription diet rich in antioxidants may help with improvement in learning ability, recognition of family members, alertness, and increased attentiveness to problem-solving tasks.
- Anipryl® (generic selegiline) is used in dogs and humans for treatment of Alzheimer's disease. Some dog owners report great improvement in their dogs, others not so much. Read the label carefully so that you can distinguish between drug side effects and normal decline in your Peke's behavior. This drug is available only by prescription.
- Cholodin, a dietary supplement, contains amino acids, vitamins, and trace minerals such as zinc and selenium. It is formulated to aid senior pets in the improvement of hearing, memory, muscle tone, alertness, and hair coat.
- Novifit®, a form of SAMe, can maintain neurotransmitter function.
- Senilife® may promote cognitive health and slow the process of decline using

As your dog approaches his senior years, your vet will be checking for signs of age-related illness.

antioxidants, including resveratrol, the substance found in red wine.

Incontinence

Females in their senior years can experience loss in bladder sphincter tone and "leak." The most common treatment is phenylpropanolmine (PPA), which causes the muscles to contract. It works in as many as 90 percent of dogs. Estrogen supplementation works in about 60 percent of dogs.

There is a surgical procedure by which the bladder is actually repositioned to reduce dribbling. In some cases, a procedure involving collagen injections can narrow the diameter of the urethra.

Bladder stones or tumors, urinary tract

infections, Cushing's disease, diabetes, and failing kidneys should be ruled out. Also consider that this may be a behavior problem, since older dogs may become more dependent on their owners and may urinate when excited to see them.

Other Aging Issues

An otherwise sweet, happy Pekingese may become aggressive as he ages. This could be due to a medical problem causing pain (arthritis or disk degeneration), vision or hearing loss, or lack of mobility. Stresses such as moving, a new family member, or a new pet may make an older dog more irritable.

Once medical causes are ruled out or treated, see whether a refresher course in simple obedience commands will help him rejuvenate. Give him plenty of praise and treats. Use a leash or halter in the house to provide more control, especially if he has decreased hearing or vision. Make sure he has stable footing and a bed he can easily get into.

It is possible your Peke needs more attention to reduce his anxiety, especially if he is blind or deaf. Try not to leave him home alone as much. Revisit that bond you built with him as a puppy or young adult! There will come a time when you will be very glad you spent that extra time with him.

While the information in this health chapter may seem overwhelming, please remember that this is just an overview of some of the out-of-the-ordinary things to watch for. When properly cared for, the Pekingese is a delightful and loveable companion who can share many years with you.

Check It Out

HEALTH CHECKLIST

✓ Find a veterinarian who is knowledgeable and kind to your Peke.
✓ Learn the signs of illness, ranging from parasites to breed-specific diseases.
✓ Follow the vaccination schedule suggested by your veterinarian.

✓ Spay or neuter your Peke to ensure the best outcome for your dog's overall health.
✓ Look into alternative therapies such as nutritional counseling and exercise.
✓ Familiarize yourself with signs of aging in your Peke, since many age-related conditions can be forestalled.

Resources

Association and Organization
Breed Clubs
American Kennel Club (AKC)
5580 Centerview Drive
Raleigh, NC 27606
Telephone: (919) 233-9767
Fax: (919) 233-3627
E-Mail: info@akc.org
www.akc.org

Canadian Kennel Club (CKC)
89 Skyway Avenue, Suite 100
Etobicoke, Ontario M9W 6R4
Telephone: (416) 675-5511
Fax: (416) 675-6506
E-Mail: information@ckc.ca
www.ckc.ca

Federation Cynologique Internationale (FCI)
Secretariat General de la FCI
Place Albert 1er, 13
B – 6530 Thuin
Belqique
www.fci.be

The Kennel Club
1 Clarges Street
London
W1J 8AB
Telephone: 0870 606 6750
Fax: 0207 518 1058
www.the-kennel-club.org.uk

The Pekingese Association, Inc.
www.pekingeseassociation.com

The Pekingese Club of America (PCA)
www.thepekingeseclubofamerica.com

United Kennel Club (UKC)
100 E. Kilgore Road
Kalamazoo, MI 49002-5584
Telephone: (269) 343-9020
Fax: (269) 343-7037
E-Mail: pbickell@ukcdogs.com
www.ukcdogs.com

Pet Sitters
National Association of Professional Pet Sitters
15000 Commerce Parkway, Suite C
Mt. Laurel, NJ 08054
Telephone: (856) 439-0324
Fax: (856) 439-0525
E-Mail: napps@ahint.com
www.petsitters.org

Pet Sitters International
201 East King Street
King, NC 27021-9161
Telephone: (336) 983-9222
Fax: (336) 983-5266
E-Mail: info@petsit.com
www.petsit.com

Rescue Organizations and Animal Welfare Groups
American Humane Association (AHA)
63 Inverness Drive East
Englewood, CO 80112
Telephone: (303) 792-9900
Fax: (303) 792-5333
www.americanhumane.org

American Society for the Prevention of Cruelty to Animals (ASPCA)
424 E. 92nd Street
New York, NY 10128-6804
Telephone: (212) 876-7700
www.aspca.org

Royal Society for the Prevention of Cruelty to Animals (RSPCA)
RSPCA Enquiries Service
Wilberforce Way, Southwater,
Horsham, West Sussex RH13 9RS
United Kingdom
Telephone: 0870 3335 999
Fax: 0870 7530 284
www.rspca.org.uk

Sports
International Agility Link (IAL)
Global Administrator: Steve Drinkwater
E-Mail: yunde@powerup.au
www.agilityclick.com/~ial

The World Canine Freestyle Organization, Inc.
P.O. Box 350122
Brooklyn, NY 11235
Telephone: (718) 332-8336
Fax: (718) 646-2686
E-Mail: WCFODOGS@aol.com
www.worldcaninefreestyle.org

Therapy
Delta Society
875 124th Ave, NE, Suite 101
Bellevue, WA 98005
Telephone: (425) 679-5500

Fax: (425) 679-5539
E-Mail: info@DeltaSociety.org
www.deltasociety.org

Therapy Dogs Inc.
P.O. Box 20227
Cheyenne WY 82003
Telephone: (877) 843-7364
Fax: (307) 638-2079
E-Mail: therapydogsinc@qwestoffice.net
www.therapydogs.com

Therapy Dogs International (TDI)
88 Bartley Road
Flanders, NJ 07836
Telephone: (973) 252-9800
Fax: (973) 252-7171
E-Mail: tdi@gti.net
www.tdi-dog.org

Training
Association of Pet Dog Trainers (APDT)
150 Executive Center Drive Box 35
Greenville, SC 29615
Telephone: (800) PET-DOGS
Fax: (864) 331-0767
E-Mail: information@apdt.com
www.apdt.com

International Association of Animal Behavior Consultants (IAABC)
565 Callery Road
Cranberry Township, PA 16066
E-Mail: info@iaabc.org
www.iaabc.org

National Association of Dog Obedience Instructors (NADOI)
PMB 369
729 Grapevine Hwy.
Hurst, TX 76054-2085
www.nadoi.org

Veterinary Associations of Animal Behavior Consultants (IAABC)
Academy of Veterinary Homeopathy (AVH)
P.O. Box 9280
Wilmington, DE 19809
Telephone: (866) 652-1590
Fax: (866) 652-1590
www.theavh.org

American Academy of Veterinary Acupuncture (AAVA)
P.O. Box 1058
Glastonbury, CT 06033
Telephone: (860) 632-9911

Fax: (860) 659-8772
www.aava.org

American Animal Hospital Association (AAHA)
12575 W. Bayaud Ave.
Lakewood, CO 80228
Telephone: (303) 986-2800
Fax: (303) 986-1700
E-Mail: info@aahanet.org
www.aahanet.org/index.cfm

American College of Veterinary Internal Medicine (ACVIM)
1997 Wadsworth Blvd., Suite A
Lakewood, CO 80214-5293
Telephone: (800) 245-9081
Fax: (303) 231-0880
Email: ACVIM@ACVIM.org
www.acvim.org

American College of Veterinary Ophthalmologists (ACVO)
P.O. Box 1311
Meridian, ID 83860
Telephone: (208) 466-7624
Fax: (208) 466-7693
E-Mail: office09@acvo.com
www.acvo.com

American Holistic Veterinary Medical Association (AHVMA)
2218 Old Emmorton Road
Bel Air, MD 21015
Telephone: (410) 569-0795
Fax: (410) 569-2346
E-Mail: office@ahvma.org
www.ahvma.org

American Veterinary Medical Association (AVMA)
1931 North Meacham Road, Suite 100
Schaumburg, IL 60173-4360
Telephone: (847) 925-8070
Fax: (847) 925-1329
E-Mail: avmainfo@avma.org
www.avma.org

ASPCA Animal Poison Control Center
Telephone: (888) 426-4435
www.aspca.org

British Veterinary Association (BVA)
7 Mansfield Street
London
W1G 9NQ
Telephone: 0207 636 6541

British Veterinary Association (BVA)
7 Mansfield Street
London
W1G 9NQ
Telephone: 0207 636 6541
Fax: 0207 908 6349
E-Mail: bvahq@bva.co.uk
www.bva.co.uk

Canine Eye Registration Foundation (CERF)
VMDB/CERF
1717 Philo Rd
PO Box 3007
Urbana, IL 61803-3007
Telephone: (217) 693-4800
Fax: (217) 693-4801
E-Mail: CERF@vmbd.org
www.vmdb.org

Orthopedic Foundation for Animals (OFA)
2300 NE Nifong Blvd
Columbus, MO 65201-3856
Telephone: (573) 442-0418
Fax: (573) 875-5073
Email: ofa@offa.org
www.offa.org

US Food and Drug Administration Center for
Veterinary Medicine (CVM)
7519 Standish Place
HFV-12
Rockville, MD 20855-0001
Telephone: (240) 276-9300 or (888) INFO-FDA
http://www.fda.gov/cvm

References
Books and Journals

Collier, V.W.F. *Dogs of China and Japan in Nature and Art.* 1921.

Dixey, Annie Coath. *The Lion Dog of Peking: Being the Astonishing History of the Pekingese Dog.* 1931.

Dodman, Nicholas, DVM. *Good Old Dog.* 2010.

Dog Watch (periodical). Cornell University College of Veterinary Medicine.

Dzanis, David A., DVM, PhD. *Vegetarian Diet for Pets.* 2009.

Godden, Rumer. *The Butterfly Lions: The Pekingese in History, Legend and Art.* 1978.

Herriot, James. *All Creatures Great and Small.* 1972.

Legl-Jacobsson, Elisabeth. *East Asiatic Breeds.* 1978.

Miller, Pat. *The Power of Positive Dog Training.* 2001.

Nicholas, Anna Katherine and Joan McDonald Brearley. *The Book of the Pekingese: From Palace Dog to the Present Day.* 1975.

Quigley, Dorothy. *The Quigley Book of the Pekingese.* 1964.

Sefton, Frances. *Pet Library's Pekingese Guide.* 1969.

The Orient Express (magazine). Doll-McGinnis Publications, 2011.

Lytton, Mrs. Neville. *Toy dogs and their ancestors, including the history and management of toy spaniels, Pekingese, Japanese, and Pomeranians.* 1911.

Your Dog (periodical). Cummings School of Veterinary Medicine at Tufts University.

Websites

American College of Veterinary Surgeons: www.acvs.org

The American Pet Products Association: www.americanpetproducts.org

Clicker Training. Karen Pryor: www.clickertraining.com

PetEducation.com: www.peteducation.com

PetPlace.com: www.petplace.com/dogs/

Tibetan Spaniel Network: www.tibbie.net/tibbies-first.html

Veterinary Practice News: www.veterinarypracticenews.com/

Vetinfo: www.vetinfo.com

WebMed: pets.webmd.com/dogs

WebVet: www.webvet.com

Nylabone www.nylabone.com

TFH Publications, Inc. www.tfh.com

Index

Note: Boldfaced numbers indicate illustrations.

Dedication
To my mom and my husband, the two people who believe in me the most.

Acknowledgments
I would like to thank Pat D'Arcy, Carrie Forsyth, and Edna Voyles for taking time to share their love for and knowledge of the Pekingese with me.

About the Author
Jenny Drastura has contributed articles to *Dog World* and *The AKC Gazette*, as well as numerous breed publications. She is a contributing writer to *The Orient Express Pekingese Magazine,* and author of the book *Shih Tzu* (Animal Planet Dogs 101). Jenny is a member of the Alliance of Purebred Dog Writers (APDW), Dog Writers Association of America (DWAA), the Society of Professional Journalists (SPJ), the American Lhasa Apso Club (ALAC), and the American Maltese Association (AMA). She has been with Marshall University in Huntington, West Virginia, in various writing capacities for the past 20 years. She is currently editor of the alumni magazine for Marshall's Joan C. Edwards School of Medicine.

She and her husband, Charlie, live with an assortment of Lhasa Apsos, Maltese, and rescues.

Photo Credits
Art_man (Shutterstock.com): 13, Bajji (Shutterstock.com): 125; Seth Casteel: 68, 98, 112, 122; Yuriy Chertok (Shutterstock.com): 76; Lars Christensen (Shutterstock.com): 35; Pat D'Arcy: 90, 103, 107, 110; Shchipkova Elena (Shutterstock.com): 82; Carrie Forsyth: 21, 22; Artem Furman (Shutterstock.com): 53, 132; Karen Givens (Shutterstock.com): 30; Igumnova Irina (Shutterstock.com): 50, 54, 81, 84; Julia Ivantsova (Shutterstock.com): 96, 126; Jagodka (Shutterstock.com): 37, 48; jovi_photo_stock (Shutterstock.com): 28; Kamira (Shutterstock.com): 24; Erik Lam (Shutterstock.com): 72, 128; lenetstan (Shutterstock.com): 116; LockStockBob (Shutterstock.com): 40; PaulShlykov (Shutterstock.com): 16; pixshots (Shutterstock.com): 73; Tatiana Popova (Shutterstock.com): 102; rebvt (Shutterstock.com): 133; Robynrg (Shutterstock.com): 4, 10, 38; Linda Schamberger: 18, 27, 101, 134; shalex84 (Shutterstock.com): 60; B. Stefanov (Shutterstock.com): 91; Val Thoermen (Shutterstock.com): 52, 130; Tish1 (Shutterstock.com): 80, 120; Graca Victoria (Shutterstock.com): 44
All other photos courtesy of Isabelle Francais and TFH archives